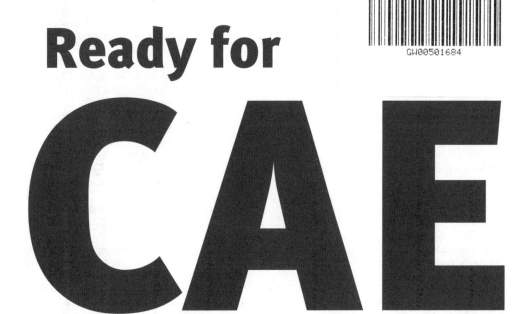

Ready for CAE

Roy Norris Amanda French

Workbook

MACMILLAN

Macmillan Education
Between Towns Road, Oxford OX4 3PP
A division of Macmillan Publishers Limited
Companies and representatives throughout the world

ISBN 1-405-01413-X (without Key)
ISBN 1-405-01412-1 (with Key)

Designed by Carolyn Gibson
Illustrated by Richard Duszczak, Peter Harper and Laszlo Veres
Cover design by Andrew Oliver

Roy Norris would like to thank Joe Wilson and Deborah Friedland for their excellent editorial work and his family, Azucena, Lara and Elisa for their support and understanding.
Amanda French would like to thank Liam Keane, and staff at Languages International, Auckland.

The publishers would like to thank Paulette Dooler, Permission Consultant for all her hard work in obtaining text permissions for this Course.

The authors and publishers would like to thank the following for permission to reproduce their material: Extract from 'Is this your idea of fun?' by Mark Mackenzie copyright © The Independent 2004, first published in The Independent 11.02.04, reprinted by permission of the publisher. Extract from 'Island hopping to a new world' by Alex Markels copyright © U.S. News & World Report, L.P 2004, first published in U.S. News & World Report 23.02.04, reprinted by permission of the publisher. Extract from 'In search of the original Teddy Bear' by Ryan Levitt copyright © The Independent 2002, first published in The Independent 27.10.02, reprinted by permission of the publisher. Extract from 'Robin Hood's escape tunnel found' by Tim Utton, first published in Daily Mail 17.08.02, reprinted by permission of Solo Syndication Limited. Extract from 'The house of maps' by Peter Whitfield, first published in Geographical Magazine December 2003, reprinted by permission of the publisher. Extract from 'No cure for the summertime blues' by Paul Gould, first published in Financial Times Weekend Section 06.09.03, reprinted by permission of the publisher. Extract from 'Ring for Ms Jeeves' by Kate Spicer copyright © N I Syndication, London 2002, first published in The Sunday Times Style Magazine 01.09.02, reprinted by permission of the publisher. Extract from 'Machine rage is dead... long live emotional computing' by Robin McKie copyright © The Observer 2004, first published in The Observer 11.04.04, reprinted by permission of the publisher. Extract from 'Marry rich... the school that teaches you how' by Julie Earle, first published in B Magazine February 2000. Extract from 'Paws for thought' by Mary Braid copyright © N I Syndication, London 2004, first published in The Sunday Times 01.02.04, reprinted by permission of the publisher. Extract from 'Noises after hours' by Luisa Dillner copyright © Luisa Dillner 1996, first published in The Guardian 23.01.96, reprinted by permission of the publisher. Extract from 'Musical genius, twins study show' by David Charter copyright © N I Syndication, London 2001, first published in The Times 09.03.01, reprinted by permission of the publisher. Extract from 'The boy who broke every rule in the book' by Scarlett Thomas copyright © The Independent 2004, first published in The Independent on Sunday 29.02.04, reprinted by permission of the publisher. Extract from 'Hospital plasters wrong leg of girl' by Sam Wallace copyright © Telegraph Group Limited 1999, first published in The Daily Telegraph 30.10.99, reprinted by permission of the publisher. Extract from 'It's so easy to work out' by Wanda Cash copyright © Telegraph Group Limited 2003, first published in The Daily Telegraph 06.02.03, reprinted by permission of the publisher. Extract from 'The truth is out there on the net' by Clive Thompson from The New Zealand Herald 05.04.04. Extract from 'Mobile-throwing contest is too close to call' by Tim Moore copyright © N I Syndication, London 2003, first published in The Times 23.08.03, reprinted by permission of the publisher. Extract from 'Technology to the ends of the earth' by Emma Bayley copyright © Focus Magazine 2000, first published in Focus Magazine January 2000, reprinted by permission of the publisher. Extract from review taken from Geographical Magazine March 2004, reprinted by permission of the publisher. Extract from review taken from Geographical Magazine September 2003, reprinted by permission of the publisher. Extract from 'Dear luggage wish you were here...' by Mark Hodson copyright © N I Syndication, London 2002, first published in The Sunday Times 25.08.02, reprinted by permission of the publisher. Extract from 'Good buy: John Felton DIY dreamer doubles his money' by by John Felton copyright © N I Syndication, London 2002, first published in The Sunday Times 01.12.02, reprinted by permission of the publisher. Extract from 'Social climbers build new life in treetops' by Tom Robbins and Geraldine Murray copyright © N I Syndication, London 2000, first published in The Sunday Times 13.02.00, reprinted by permission of the publisher. Extract from 'My Paris' copyright © The Independent 2004, first published in The Independent 21.03.04, reprinted by permission of the publisher. Extract from 'See the world and change your life' by Jill Toddy first published in Saga Magazine April 2003, reprinted by permission of the publisher. Extract from 'Hippo heaven' by Mark Deeble copyright © Mark Deeble 2003, first published in BBC Wildlife February 2003, reprinted by permission of the publisher. Extract from 'Mysterious case of the piranha that fell from the sky' by Arifa Akbar copyright © The Independent 2004, first published in The Independent 21.02.04, reprinted by permission of the publisher. Extract from Rainforest Concern advertisement: We have a choice, reprinted by permission of the publisher. Extract from 'The power to change' copyright © The Independent 2002, first published in The Independent 30.03.02, reprinted by permission of the publisher. Extract from 'Give them stick' by John Lichfield copyright © The Independent 2004, first published in The Independent 24.03.04, reprinted by permission of the publisher. Extract from 'Britain is the ready-meal glutton' by Anthony Browne copyright © N I Syndication, London 2003, first published in The Times 21.02.03, reprinted by permission of the publisher. Extract from 'Superfoods that heal' by Anne Montague copyright © National Magazine Company 2002, first published in Good Housekeeping Magazine August 2002, reprinted by permission of the publisher. Extract from 'Elderly lose £40 million in distraction burglaries' by John Steele copyright © Telegraph Group Limited 2001, first published in The Daily Telegraph 28.12.01, reprinted by permission of the publisher. Extract from 'Who needs money when you've got a spring in your step?' by Hermoine Eyre copyright © The Independent 2004, first published in The Independent 17.03.04, reprinted by permission of the publisher. Extract from 'The joys of modern life' by Rachel Ragg copyright © The Independent 1999, first published in The Independent 21.12.99, reprinted by permission of the publisher. Extract from 'After the celebrations have ended' by Margaret E Ward copyright © N I Syndication, London 2002, first published in The Sunday Times 31.03.02, reprinted by permission of the publisher.

Disclaimer:
Although every effort has been made to contact copyright holders before publication, this has not always been possible. If notified, the publisher undertakes to rectify any errors or omissions at the earliest opportunity.

The authors and publishers would like to thank the following for permission to reproduce their photographs:
Alamy pp20, 44, 81; Corbis p4, Corbis/Corbis/Christie's Images p16, Michael S Lewis p9, Corbis/José Luis Pelaez p32, Corbis/Davis Raymer p58; Corbis R.F p84; Image Bank p72; Photodisc Green p9; Rainforest Concern p96.

Cover and title page photos provided by
Thinkstock, Digital Vision, Photodisk

Printed and bound in Spain by Edelvives.

2008 2007 2006 2005
10 9 8 7 6 5 4 3 2

Contents

Reading

CAE Part 1

Multiple matching

1 Read the article about the explorer Ranulph Fiennes quickly. In the article, is he mainly

A giving advice to inexperienced explorers?
B talking about the nature of exploration?
C promoting adventure travel to young people?

2 For questions **1–14**, answer by choosing from the sections of the article (**A–G**). Some of the choices may be required more than once.

In which section are the following mentioned?

the suggestion that Fiennes still seems enthusiastic about exploration	1 ____
an aspect of Fiennes's character that has been unfairly highlighted	2 ____
a negative effect of the growing interest in adventure travel	3 ____
a reason Fiennes gives for exploration becoming more attractive to amateurs	4 ____
a misconception regarding the knowledge previous explorers had	5 ____
Fiennes's fascination with a field in which he is relatively inexperienced	6 ____
people with normal fitness being able to cope with certain expeditions	7 ____
disapproval of explorers having too much respect for their own field	8 ____
the view that only professional explorers were capable of reaching distant destinations	9 ____
the instinctive human desire to explore new places	10 ____
the suggestion that more care is taken on difficult routes	11 ____
Fiennes's primary motivation for being an explorer	12 ____
the importance given by explorers to a certain kind of achievement	13 ____
Fiennes being held in high regard by other adventurers	14 ____

IS THIS YOUR IDEA OF FUN?

Sir Ranulph Fiennes is the world's greatest living explorer. But now it seems an endless stream of people are conquering the South Pole or clambering up Everest. Mark MacKenzie asks him, is the exploring game becoming too easy?

A

In the field of human exploration, Sir Ranulph Fiennes's personal achievements are remarkable. Discovering lost desert cities, navigating uncharted channels of the White Nile; in more than 30 years in the adventure business he has done the lot. Numerous expeditions to the North and South Poles have turned him into an iconic figure, the explorer's explorer. Now there are many amateurs that would follow in his footsteps. Adventure travel is one of the fastest growing sectors of the travel market. Offering trips to destinations including Mount Everest, Antarctica and the South Pole, tour companies can now provide access for those less tough to remote parts of the planet once considered the exclusive playgrounds of experts such as Fiennes and his peers.

B

This year, record numbers are expected at the base camp of Everest all hoping to reach the summit of the world's tallest peak. So, is the exploring game getting too easy? "Anyone who plans carefully could get to the South Pole if they're in relatively good condition and go at the right time of year," says Fiennes. "I would say the same of Mount Everest. If the weather's good and you take a reasonable guide, you should be able to get up even if you've never climbed before. However, there are still plenty of expeditions the majority of the public would not be able to do. Crossing the whole continent of Antarctica unsupported, for example, your troubles only really start at the South Pole. But the urge to go to far-flung regions is innate to man," Fiennes continues, "and I think provided there is no ecological damage, this is fine. On Everest though, there has been a dramatic impact in terms of litter."

C

But with specialist companies willing to deposit increasing numbers of tourists in ever more remote locations, is exploring becoming just an exercise in logistics, rather than a true test of character? "The challenge is what you make of it," says Fiennes. "In the wrong weather, you can have the most horrendous time on reasonably easy routes. But the ratio of accidents on challenging ones such as Everest or at the South Pole is lesser than those on certain tourist routes, because you expect to be very cold and encounter crevasses." Also lying behind the increasing numbers of extreme adventurers, says Fiennes, is the improved technology used for polar equipment. "It's all a lot lighter now, less bulky. If you're inexperienced, that makes these journeys a lot more appealing

D

Patrick Woodhead, whose young team reached the South Pole in 75 days, believes the explorer community has a tendency to be overly reverential towards their discipline and claims his South Pole trek was a thoroughly enjoyable experience. However, last year, Fiennes published a biography of the original Antarctic explorer, Captain Robert Falcon Scott, and he feels there are those among modern explorers who remain ignorant of the debt they owe to Scott's pioneering spirit. "People today think we knew back then that Antarctica was a continent – we didn't. On his first expedition to Antarctica in 1902, Scott made an 800-mile journey when the furthest expedition previously had been 14 miles."

E

What is it that has driven explorers to the extremes of the Earth? "Explorers have always had a thousand different motives," Fiennes acknowledges. "If these weren't noble, they would never admit it. If I'm asked myself, I am quite clear. It's my profession and how I make an income. There are people who aren't comfortable with that. I'm supposed to say "Because it's there to be conquered." I think some people still need this image of nobility." Such frankness has contributed to Fiennes's reputation for occasional haughtiness. On an expedition in 1971, he made the mistake of taking along a television crew. "It meant good publicity for future expeditions," he says. "but they deliberately set out with the aim of showing me up as a dictator."

F

Nevertheless, Fiennes has built his reputation on the only sort of accomplishment that matters among his peers – being first. "When Sir Edmund Hillary first scaled Everest, he used every aid at his disposal. The next 'first' then has to be the person to do it without oxygen, then the first solo ascent and so on." So are there any true 'firsts' left? "In part, it's the attitude of the individual," he says. "If something has been done, they will find their own firsts. Eventually, expeditions end up relying on gimmicks; the first person to the South Pole on a motorbike, then the first on a camel and so on."

G

In 1992, Fiennes completed his first archaeological expedition to find the lost city of Ubar in the deserts of Oman. He admits he found the detective work intriguing, albeit a challenge for a relative amateur, and believes the possibility of making similar discoveries may increasingly occupy his time in the future. He will be sixty in March and his appetite for adventure and discovery appears undiminished. Last November, he and Mike Stroud became the first men to run seven marathons in seven countries in as many days. Is adventuring getting too easy? Not just yet.

Vocabulary

Wordlist on page 209 of the Coursebook.

Verb and noun collocations

Complete each of the gaps with one of the words from the box.

out	with	in	to	into

1 Their solar panel business **ran** _____ **problems** after a succession of wet summers in the mid-nineteen nineties.

2 Last year's police campaign to reduce the number of accidents on motorways **met** _____ **limited success**.

3 Union leaders have not **ruled** _____ **the possibility of** taking strike action.

4 Her attempt to cycle across the Sahara **ended** _____ **failure** yesterday, when she fell off her bike and broke her leg.

5 Taking on the Cup holders was no easy task, but they **rose** _____ **the challenge** and drew 1–1.

Adjective and noun collocations

1 One of the items of vocabulary in each group is not normally used with the word in capitals. Cross out the item which does not fit. There is an example at the beginning (0).

0	distinct	~~heavy~~	remote	strong	**POSSIBILITY**
1	fair	inside	realistic	slim	**CHANCE**
2	potential	recurrent	resounding	trivial	**PROBLEM**
3	burning	daunting	exciting	fresh	**CHALLENGE**
4	hard	high	personal	poor	**MOTIVATION**
5	huge	overnight	roaring	terrible	**SUCCESS**
6	continued	dismal	inevitable	urgent	**FAILURE**
7	heated	lifelong	greatest	secret	**AMBITION**
8	major	outlying	remarkable	sporting	**ACHIEVEMENT**

2 Complete each space with an appropriate adjective from exercise 1. There is an example at the beginning (0).

0 I can't understand why he applied for the job; there was**n't even a** _remote_ **possibility** that he'd get it.

1 Recent corruption scandals mean that the party now stands **only a** _____ **chance of** victory in the forthcoming elections.

2 During his adolescence, serious illness was a _____ **problem**, and always seemed to strike at exam time.

3 The situation does pose **a rather** _____ **challenge**, but we will not be put off.

4 His consistently low marks seem to be both the result and the cause of _____ **motivation**.

5 The book brought her great wealth and worldwide fame, but this was **no** _____ **success**; her previous two novels had been bestsellers in her own country.

6 It was a night of _____ **failure** for British athletes, whose recent successes had given cause for great optimism.

7 As I've always said, it's been a _____ **ambition** of mine to play Hamlet, and now at last I can fulfil it.

8 Undoubtedly, the greatest _____ **achievement** of the year was Alek Schmidt's record-breaking marathon run of two hours and four minutes.

Word formation

Complete each gap with an appropriate noun form of the word in capitals at the end of the line. There is an example at the beginning **(0)**.

Don't forget!

You may need to use the negative or plural form of the noun.

0 Many people at the club are questioning the _wisdom_ of signing the 16-year-old goalkeeper.   **WISE**

1 Excessive _____ to direct sunlight should of course be avoided.   **EXPOSE**

2 Councillors have once again rejected _____ for a new multi-storey car park.   **PROPOSE**

3 Management criticized the unions for their stubborn attitude and _____ in the wage negotiations.   **FLEXIBLE**

4 The government is concerned at the number of unfilled _____ in the nursing profession.   **VACANT**

5 There is a strong feeling within the company that greater _____ should be placed on staff development.   **EMPHASIZE**

6 Failure to meet legal safety _____ has led to the temporary closure of the fairground.   **REQUIRE**

7 She chose to live in Brighton because of its mild climate and _____ to London.   **CLOSE**

8 There is a chronic _____ of housing in our cities.   **SHORT**

9 The complete _____ of this answer shows that the candidate did not read the question carefully.   **RELEVANT**

10 He achieved _____ for failing a drugs test after winning an Olympic final.   **NOTORIOUS**

Language focus

 Grammar reference on page 216 of the Coursebook.

Spelling

The following letter contains **20** spelling mistakes. Find the mistakes and correct them.

Dear Sir,

I am writting to complain about an article that apeared in the 'Winners and Loosers' section in last weekend's edition of your newspaper.

The article, wich analyses the growth of my educational publishing company, 'ABC', describes me as 'a man with surprisingly little education' and attributes my success to 'agresive ambition and a complete disregard for the wellfare of his employees'. This is, of course, totaly untrue, and althought I do not intend to justify myself or my business methods, their are one or two observations I feel I ough to make.

Firstly, the economics degree I obtained from Bristol University speaks for itself, particularly, I feel, as I graduated with first class honours. In adition, whilst I am

proud to consider myself ambitious, this is not at the expense of my staff, who would, I know, be only too pleased for you to intervue them. Indeed, they would be disappointed if they where not given the oportunity to inform your readers of their generous salary, impresive working conditions and excellent promotion prospects.

As you can imagine, your article has caused considerable pane and embarrassment, both too myself and my family, who found it extremly upsetting. I trust you will print an apology in the next edition of your newspaper, pointing out and rectifying the innacuracies in the article.

Yours faithfuly

John Austin

Modal verbs: *might, could, may, can*

1 In **1–7**, complete the second sentence so that it has the same meaning as the first. There is an example at the beginning **(0)**.

0 Would you mind lending me your pen for a moment?
May *I borrow your pen for a moment* ?

1 Although he lives here, we never see him.
He may _____ .

2 They're very likely to ask you to speak French during the interview.
You may _____ .

3 Perhaps she didn't know you were married.
She might _____ .

4 He had a good chance of getting the job, but he didn't apply.
If he'd applied for the job, he could _____ .

5 I rarely use my bike these days, so it would make sense if I sold it.
I rarely use my bike these days, so I may _____ .

6 Why on earth didn't you tell me you were vegetarian?
You might _____ !

7 It's unlikely she was enjoying herself very much.
She can't _____ .

I rarely use my bike these days, so it would make sense if I sold it!

2 In **1–7**, one of the three alternatives is incorrect. Cross it out. There is an example at the beginning **(0)**.

0 You ~~might not~~/may not/cannot leave until I give you permission.

1 It's not my scarf – I think it *might/could/can* be Graham's.

2 It *might/may/could* not be warm enough to eat outside tonight, but we'll keep our fingers crossed.

3 He's so lazy – he *might/may/could* at least offer to do the washing up!

4 I know you didn't want to come, but you *might/may/could* as well try and enjoy yourself now that you're here.

5 Don't run across the road like that again – you *might/may/could* have been run over!

6 It was a tough walk, but we *could/were able to/managed to* reach the end before it got dark.

7 Police are now saying that the fire *might/may/could* not have been started deliberately, although they have refused to rule out the possibility of arson entirely.

English in Use

CAE Part 1

Multiple-choice cloze

For questions **1–15**, read the text below and then decide which answer **A**, **B**, **C** or **D** best fits each space. The exercise begins with an example **(0)**.

On top of the world

In May 1998, just two years after breaking his back in a parachuting accident whilst **(0)** ___ in the army, Bear Grylls became the youngest Briton to **(1)** ___ the summit of Mount Everest and return **(2)** ___ . He was just 23 years old.

As his back recovered and he regained his **(3)** ___ , Bear decided to leave the army in order to **(4)** ___ his lifelong ambition to conquer the highest **(5)** ___ in the world. A friend of his was organising an expedition to Everest and Bear asked to **(6)** ___ . After a year spent preparing for the climb and **(7)** ___ sponsorship money, he and his companions moved out to the Himalayas to **(8)** ___ up the challenge.

In **(9)** ___ Bear spent over 10 weeks on the mountain's south-east face. This **(10)** ___ a whole week at Camp Two simply waiting for the right **(11)** ___ to make his attempt on the summit. When he finally made it to the top, he sat for 20 minutes, just gazing in wonder at the **(12)** ___ before him.

The hardest part was still to come though. Every year the number of climbers killed on Everest increases, with most deaths **(13)** ___ on the descent. It is **(14)** ___ surprising then, that Bear should feel a **(15)** ___ sense of relief when he eventually got back to base camp. Three British climbers under 25 have tried to conquer Everest; Bear is the only one to survive.

0 A assisting	**B** obeying	**C** ordering	**D** <u>serving</u>
1 A achieve	**B** reach	**C** get	**D** attain
2 A live	**B** lively	**C** living	**D** alive
3 A power	**B** force	**C** vigour	**D** strength
4 A hunt	**B** chase	**C** pursue	**D** trace
5 A crest	**B** pinnacle	**C** peak	**D** tip
6 A join	**B** unite	**C** attach	**D** link
7 A rising	**B** raising	**C** arising	**D** arousing
8 A take	**B** rise	**C** face	**D** put
9 A summary	**B** short	**C** total	**D** conclusion
10 A contained	**B** included	**C** comprised	**D** consisted
11 A states	**B** conditions	**C** events	**D** stages
12 A eyesight	**B** outlook	**C** vision	**D** view
13 A emerging	**B** going on	**C** occurring	**D** unfolding
14 A barely	**B** equally	**C** rarely	**D** hardly
15 A great	**B** large	**C** wide	**D** full

Writing

Competition entries

1 Read the following Writing Part 2 task.

You see the following announcement in an international magazine for young people.

Competition

Everyone has achieved something at some time in their life, whether it's learning to swim, passing an exam or running a marathon. Write and tell us about one of your own personal achievements, no matter how great or small. You should write about:

● your reasons for wanting to achieve this goal

● the preparations you made

● the feelings you experienced.

The best entry will win a year's subscription to this magazine.

2 Read the model answer below and choose the most attractive and appropriate title, **A, B, C** or **D**.

A Rebecca
B Stage fright
C An overnight success
D The beginning of a long acting career

Acting can be a nerve-racking experience at the best of times, but when you're playing a lead role made famous by the great Laurence Olivier, the feeling may well be something approaching intense fear. That, at least, was the case for me when I appeared as Maxim de Winter in an amateur production of 'Rebecca' by Daphne du Maurier.

Why, you might ask, would anyone willingly put themselves through such an ordeal? It seemed so obvious at the time. I'd been involved in amateur dramatics for three or four years, but I'd only ever been given minor parts or supporting roles and my motivation was beginning to run low. So when I was offered the chance to head the cast in the stage version of du Maurier's classic, I felt more than ready to take up the challenge.

When rehearsals started though, I began to wish I hadn't been quite so keen to accept the part. There were one or two very tricky monologues, which, just thinking about them now, still cause me to have butterflies in my stomach. I spent hours at home practising in front of the mirror, trying out different postures, experimenting with a range of gestures and varying the tone of my voice in a thousand ways.

On the night of the first performance, my legs were trembling and my shirt was soaked with sweat. But I got through it. The play enjoyed a reasonable degree of success and a review in the local newspaper described my contribution as 'convincing'. Naturally, I was delighted and I was almost tempted to audition for the part of Sherlock Holmes in an adaptation of 'The Hound of the Baskervilles'. Almost.

3   The task asks writers to include information on three aspects of their achievement: their reasons, preparations and feelings.

In which paragraph (or paragraphs) is each of these aspects mentioned?

4   In the last paragraph, the writer varies the length of the sentences. What is the purpose of this?

5   Find examples in the model of each of the following features of more informal writing.

Contractions eg *don't*

Phrasal verbs eg *give up*

Informal words linking sentences eg *And*

Addressing the reader directly eg *you*

6   The writer uses a variety of past tenses to narrate the events leading up to the achievement. Find examples of different past tenses.

7   Now write your own answer to the task. Before you do so, read the **Don't forget box** and do the exercise in the **Useful language box** below.

Don't forget!

- Plan your answer before you write.
- Address all the points in the task.
- Engage the reader's interest in the first paragraph.
- Use a range of tenses and vocabulary.
- Write in a consistent register.
- Give your entry a title.

Useful language

The expressions in the box are either informal or neutral. Put each one in the appropriate column according to its meaning. The first one has been done for you.

~~have butterflies in your stomach~~	be over the moon	be/get uptight
be/feel down	be/feel on top of the world	be a bundle of nerves
be on a high	feel sorry for yourself	be as pleased as punch
be/feel panicky	be in low spirits	

Nervous	Happy	Sad
have butterflies in your stomach		

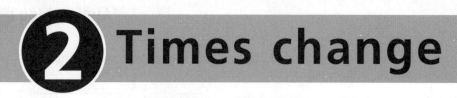

Times change

CAE Part 3

Multiple choice

Read the following magazine article about the first people to arrive in the Americas. Answer questions **1–6** by choosing a letter **A, B, C** or **D**. Give only one answer to each question.

Island hopping to a new world

Digging in a dank limestone cave in Canada's Queen Charlotte Islands last summer, Christina Heaton hardly noticed the triangular piece of chipped stone she'd unearthed in a pile of debris. Then, as her scientist father, Timothy, sifted through the muck, he realized her unwitting find was actually invaluable. It was a spear point. Bear bones found near the artefact indicated its owner had presumably speared the beast, which later retreated into the cave and eventually died with the point still lodged in its loins. Radiocarbon tests soon dated the remains at about 12,000 years old, making them the earliest signs of human activity in the region or, for that matter, in all of the Americas.

Almost from the moment the first white explorers set eyes on America's indigenous 'Indians', people have wondered where they came from. Fray José Acosta, a Jesuit priest, was one of the first to make a sensible conjecture in 1590 that a small group from Asia's northernmost latitudes must have walked to the New World. Indeed, since the 1930s archaeologists have taught that the first Americans were hunters who crossed the Bering land bridge from Siberia, chasing mammoths southward through Canada down a narrow corridor between two ice sheets. By about 11,500 years ago, they'd got as far as Clovis, New Mexico, near where archaeologists first found their distinctive spear points. Their descendants ultimately reached the tip of South America after a footslogging journey begun more than 20,000 miles away. Or so the story goes.

Yet the Heatons' find is the latest addition to a small but weighty pile of tools and remains suggesting the first Americans may have come from Asia not down the centre of the continent but along the coast in boats, centuries or millenniums prior to the Clovis people. The evidence that Heaton and his colleagues are seeking has turned up along the Pacific coast all the way from Alaska to southern Chile. So far it does not include any human remains of pre-Clovis age, but a woman's bones were found on Santa Rosa Island off the Californian coast. While the bones show that the woman herself was alive 200-300 years after the Clovis people's long trek, it is likely that she was the descendant of earlier settlers. And scientists excavating Chile's Monte Verde site, over 6,000 miles from the southernmost Clovis find, have discovered medicinal herbs and artefacts that date back over 12,500 years.

Such finds have backed up genetic and biological research to paint a far more complex picture of America's first explorers. Rather than a single migration of Clovis people, "there were clearly several waves of human exploration," says Douglas Wallace, a geneticist at the University of California-Irvine. Wallace's DNA studies of American natives identify at least five genetically distinct waves, four from Asia and one possibly of early European descent, the earliest of which could have arrived more than 20,000 years ago. That diversity concurs with research by linguists who argue the Americas' 143 native languages couldn't have all developed from a single 115,000-year-old tongue. And if they had, then the languages would be the most diverse along the mainland route the Clovis people travelled. In fact, the number of languages is greatest along the Pacific coast, adding to suspicions that at least some of the first immigrants came that way.

Until recently, many geologists assumed that the Ice-Age shore was a glaciated wasteland. But new studies of fossils and ancient climates imply a navigable coastline full of shellfish and other foods, with grassy inland tundra capable of supporting big game – and perhaps sea-faring humans heading south. Unfortunately, looking for evidence that could clinch the coastal-migration scenario is akin to searching for the mythical sunken city of Atlantis. Warming temperatures since the last Ice Age have transformed the ancient tundra into thick forests, rendering most signs of early human exploration all but invisible, and melting Ice-Age glaciers have submerged most of the coastal campsites where the ancient mariners may have sojourned.

In 1998, archaeologist Daryl Fedje retrieved an ancient hunting blade, one of the first human artefacts found in the region. This inspired some to call for a comprehensive high-tech search of the sea floor yet the immense costs of a seafloor survey have prevented this. So Fedje and other researchers have instead focused on caves on the nearby islands and in Alaska, where artefacts are protected from weather and decay. "The caves have been a real windfall," says Heaton of the animal bones he has found. He's confident that it's just a matter of time before he and his colleagues find pre-Clovis human remains because "in almost every cave we put our shovels to, we find something new."

Don't forget!

The questions follow the same order as the information in the text.

1 When Timothy Heaton noticed the spear point, he was
   A certain that an important discovery had been made.
   B reluctant to speculate how it had arrived in the cave.
   C surprised to find such an artefact located in that area.
   D disappointed that it was not something more significant.

2 What are we told about archaeologists in the 1930s?
   A They disputed José Acosta's theory about the origins of native Americans.
   B They believed that the first migrants made their long trek on foot.
   C They were the first to suggest a migration pattern beginning in Canada.
   D They were unaware of the distance that early hunters had really travelled.

3 What point is exemplified by the references to the find on Santa Rosa Island?
   A The Clovis people could have had the ability to build primitive boats.
   B The Clovis people were the earliest of the migrant groups to explore the coast.
   C Migrants may have been on the island before Clovis groups were on the mainland.
   D Descendants of the Clovis people must have spread out in search of new territory.

4 The research that Douglas Wallace has carried out
   A shows early migrants were more sophisticated than previously thought.
   B indicates that the first settlers in America were most likely from Europe.
   C suggests that the Clovis people had reached America over 20,000 years ago.
   D supports the argument proposed by linguists about native American languages.

5 What does the writer state about the possible route that early migrants took?
   A The Ice Age had little significant impact on the American coastline.
   B It is virtually impossible to find proof of migration on this route.
   C The early travellers probably chose this route for its food supplies.
   D Certain archaeologists are looking for a route that never existed.

6 Timothy Heaton decided to excavate caves in the Queen Charlotte Islands because
   A a thorough exploration of the sea bed is not feasible.
   B his research team are in direct competition with Fedje's.
   C human remains have already been found in this location.
   D there may another layer of artefacts under the Clovis layer.

Vocabulary

Wordlist on page 210 of the Coursebook.

Changes

1 For questions **1–4**, complete each of the gaps with a word from the box. The verb you choose must be appropriate for the gaps in both sentences. There is an example at the beginning **(0)**.

| adapted |
| altered |
| shifted |
| transferred |

0 a I've _changed_ **my mind** – I'll have the soup instead of the prawn cocktail.
   b He _changed_ **places with** Jean so that he could sit nearer the blackboard.

1 a Football star David Beckham was _____ from Manchester United to Real Madrid **for a fee of** £25 million.
   b I've just _____ £3,000 from my current account to my savings account.

2 a When asked why he hadn't done his homework, James _____ **uncomfortably in his seat**.
   b The publishing company has _____ **its attention away from** children's literature **towards** school text books.

3 a The snow leopard has _____ **to life** at altitudes of up to 6,000 metres.
   b Several of her **books** have been _____ **for television**.

4 a The jacket was a perfect fit, but I **had the trousers** _____ because they were a little too tight.
   b The new tower block has dramatically _____ **the appearance** of the town.

2 Underline the word **A, B, C** or **D** which best fits each space.

1 He's _____ changed at all since I last saw him – just as lively and outgoing as he always was.

    A slightly   **B** hardly   **C** subtly   **D** nearly

2 The seat is _____ adjusted by pulling on this lever here.

    A highly   **B** fully   **C** openly   **D** easily

3 Prices vary _____ , so do shop around before you buy your barbecue.

    A widely   **B** instantly   **C** completely   **D** closely

4 In response to growing criticism, the government modified its plans for education cuts, though only very _____ .

    A barely   **B** fundamentally   **C** slightly   **D** faintly

5 To her credit, she _____ transformed the business from a string of small shops into a major international chain of department stores.

    A radically   **B** revoltingly   **C** enormously   **D** increasingly

3 Complete each of the gaps with one of the words from the box.

fortunes	heart	scene	pace	condition	attitudes	direction	law

1 You should go away somewhere for the weekend. **A change of** _____ will do you good.

2 At first my parents refused to let me go off travelling on my own, but then they **had a change of** _____ .

3 After a very slow start, the car chase gives the film **a** much needed **change of** _____ .

4 In **a complete change of** _____ he gave up his job in teaching and became a farmer.

5 The win **marked a change in the** _____ of the team, which had lost its previous six games.

6 Despite the operation on his eye, there has been **no significant change in the patient's** _____ .

7 Anti-smoking campaigners yesterday **called for a change in the** _____ to make it illegal for people to smoke in bars and cafés.

8 The legalization of divorce reflected **a change in** _____ **towards** marriage.

Self help

Add the expressions in bold in exercise 3 to your vocabulary notebook.

He gave up his job in teaching and became a farmer.

Language focus

 Grammar reference on page 216 of the Coursebook.

1 Correct the following sentences by changing the underlined word or words. You may need to write more than one word. There is an example at the beginning **(0)**.

have known

0 I <u>know</u> him since we were at school together.

1 We <u>would</u> have a parrot, but he flew away one day when I was cleaning his cage.

2 The service was terrible; when our dessert arrived, Paul still <u>ate</u> his starter!

3 I <u>have met</u> some very interesting people on my holiday last year.

4 This must be about the tenth time I <u>eat</u> in this restaurant.

5 It's a long time since we <u>don't see</u> each other.

6 It wasn't the first time she <u>was catching</u> him taking money from her purse.

7 I'd like to <u>stay</u> in London longer, but we had to get back for Sandra's wedding.

8 I'd rather you <u>didn't give</u> him my phone number – he phoned me three times yesterday!

9 You <u>did</u> nothing but complain since we've been here.

10 She was about <u>sitting</u> down, when she noticed the chair was broken.

2 Complete each of the gaps with an appropriate tense or form of the verb in brackets.

A

Derek Taylor, 87, is one of Britain's longest-serving Santas: he **(1)** _____ (put) on his red suit and white beard for nearly 50 years now. He believes he **(2)** _____ (manage) to hold down his job in a Rotherham department store for so long by adapting to the changing attitudes of the children he **(3)** _____ (meet) down the years. "Back in the 1950s, children **(4)** _____ (believe) in Father Christmas totally and **(5)** _____ (ask) lots of questions, like 'Where exactly do you live?' or 'How do you manage to squeeze down chimneys?' Nowadays they just tell me about the presents they want. Of course, the toys they ask for **(6)** _____ (change) dramatically over the years. In the old days, if you **(7)** _____ (say) you would try and bring them the doll or roller skates they wanted, their faces **(8)** _____ (light) up. Now it's all mobile phones, computers and DVD players."

B

I'll never forget the time I **(1)** _____ (go) to the hairdresser's in the early 1950s for my first perm, or 'permanent wave', after I **(2)** _____ (see) a picture of Gina Lollobrigida with one in a film magazine. I **(3)** _____ (work) in a shop at the time, and I **(4)** _____ (book) an appointment for 1.30 pm on Wednesday afternoon, my half day off. **(5)** _____ (wash) and cut my hair, the hairdresser rolled it into tight and rather painful metal curlers. He then connected the curlers to wires from a machine that looked as if it **(6)** _____ (just/land) from outer space! He chose that moment to tell me he **(7)** _____ (experience) problems with the machine for the last few days and that the 'baking' procedure **(8)** _____ (take) a little longer than expected. In fact, I **(9)** _____ (spend) over 6 hours in the hairdresser's altogether and **(10)** _____ (not/arrive) home until well after 8 o'clock! At one point during my long ordeal, after I **(11)** _____ (sit) in the same chair for about 4 hours, my worried husband phoned the hairdresser's to ask what time I **(12)** _____ (leave). It was the first time I **(13)** _____ (ever/have) a perm, and I decided there and then that it **(14)** _____ (be) my last!

English in Use

Error correction

In **most** lines of the following text, there is **either** a spelling **or** a punctuation error. For each numbered line **1–16**, write the correctly spelled word or show the correct punctuation at the end of the line. Some lines are correct. Indicate these lines with a tick (✔). The exercise begins with three examples (**0**), (**00**) and (**000**).

Don't forget!

There are never more than five correct lines in a text.

The Teddy Bear

0	Although teddy bears can be found, all around the world, you have	*found all*
00	to go to the little town of Giengen in Germany to trace the routes	*roots*
000	of this cuddly toy. Giengen is the home of the Steiff Manufacturing	✓
1	Company, where Richard Steiff, drew and produced the world's	_____
2	first jointed toy bear in 1902. But how did they come up with	_____
3	the name Teddy. According to legend, the former US President	_____
4	Theodore Roosevelt once went hunting in Mississippi. He was	_____
5	unable to shoot anything during his trip, so locals tyed a bear to	_____
6	a tree to help him bag a prize. His refusal to shoot the helpless	_____
7	animal inspired New York shopkeeper's Morris and Rose Michtom	_____
8	to start producing commemorative "Teddy Bears" Germany may	_____
9	have made the first ones, but americans came up with the name.	_____
10	Teddy bears are still made at the Steiff factery in Giengen, and	_____
11	tourists can visit the site where the best friends and silent confidants	_____
12	of many children are produced. Steiff also has a museum in wich	_____
13	some of the world's most important teddies are gathered. Situated	_____
14	inside a squat, glass biulding designed by Richard Steiff, the structure	_____
15	is a temple to teddydom with more than five hundred bears on dissplay	_____
16	at any one time, drawn from an archive of at least fivteen thousand.	_____

CAE Part 4 **Word formation**

For questions **1–15**, use the words in the boxes to the right of the texts to form **one** word that fits the same numbered space in the text. The exercise begins with an example **(0)**.

Robin Hood: fact or fiction?

The **(0)** _discovery_ of a secret tunnel beneath a Nottingham museum could prove that one of history's most famous legends was a flesh-and-blood reality. The tunnel may have been used by Robin Hood to escape from the Sheriff of Nottingham to the **(1)** _____ of Sherwood Forest. For centuries **(2)** _____ have questioned the **(3)** _____ of Robin, dismissing him as a romanticized figure who **(4)** _____ the hopes of the poor in their struggle against the rich. The **(5)** _____ unearthing of the passageway by archaeologists excavating some man-made caves may cause them to rethink their views. The tunnel is blocked so its exact length is **(6)** _____ , though it could stretch for three miles, from St Mary's Church to the city's outskirts. According to medieval documents, Robin and his men **(7)** _____ disappeared from the church after being surrounded there by the Sheriff's soldiers.

0	DISCOVER
1	SAFE
2	HISTORY
3	EXIST
4	SYMBOL
5	ACCIDENT
6	KNOW
7	MYSTERY

Book review: 'Walls have ears' by Mark Mitchell

Avid **(8)** _____ of Mark Mitchell's historical novels will not be disappointed by his **(9)** _____ offering, 'Walls have ears', a simple, but **(10)** _____ written tale of childhood innocence in a world of adult corruption. Mitchell shot to fame thanks to the television **(11)** _____ of his fourth novel, 'Baroque of Ages', which followed the fortunes of two teenage siblings in seventeenth-century Britain. Despite the author's **(12)** _____ with the TV production, **(13)** _____ Marian Blackshaw and Edek Sobera, it was a huge success and **(14)** _____ of his books for children rocketed overnight. 'Walls have ears' is a **(15)** _____ on the central theme of 'Baroque of Ages', though this time, set against the background of Hadrian's Wall at the time of its construction in the second century.

8	READ
9	LATE
10	BEAUTY
11	ADAPT
12	SATISFY
13	STAR
14	SELL
15	VARY

Writing

CAE Part 1

Formal and informal letters

1 Read the following Writing Part 1 task.

You have just been on a week's historical tour of Rome, booked with the travel agency Timson's Tours. Overall, you were very pleased with the holiday, though certain aspects of the tour have prompted you to write to Timson's and recommend some changes. A friend of yours who is going on a Timson's Tour to Rome next month has written to you asking you how you enjoyed your holiday and whether you can pass on any useful information.

Read the magazine advertisement and the testimonials from Timson's website, on which you have made some notes, and the extract from the letter from your friend. Then, **using the information appropriately**, write:

a a **letter** to your friend giving your overall opinion of the tour, explaining which aspects were not satisfactory and giving advice on how to prepare for the holiday.

b a **letter** to Timson's Tours giving your overall opinion of the tour, explaining which aspects were not satisfactory and making recommendations for improvements.

You should use your own words as far as possible.

Timson's *Historical Tours*

Rome, the Eternal City

Explore the city's past with one of our specialist guides, who will bring the history of ancient Rome alive for you. Our seven-day itinerary will take you to some of the best known historical sites of the Eternal City, including:

 The Pantheon: possibly the most intact building from antiquity anywhere in the world

 The Colosseum: the enormous ancient Roman sports arena

 The Sistine Chapel: Michelangelo's masterpiece, considered by many to be the greatest work of art ever created

 A coach trip to the ancient Roman port of Ostia, arrival point for the empire's riches, which were taken up the Tiber to Rome — *didn't get there – coach broke down*

Palatine Hill: one of the seven hills of Rome, where Romulus and Remus were found by the she-wolf that kept them alive

three – guide sick on last day

There will also be two free days for you to do your own exploring with the help of our excellent guidebook, provided free to all participants. — *not the word I'd use*

The cost of the trip is £1,600, and includes return flights, four-star accommodation with bed and breakfast near the Spanish Steps and coach trips in and around Rome. — *but not cost of admission to monuments!*

We were most impressed by the range of sites we visited, and the guide was first class. She certainly knew what she was talking about and she made it all sound so interesting. — *sounds like our guide*

Amy and Fred Woodcock, York, England

Bravissimo! Our guide, Maria, was superb, and the guidebook we were given for our two free days was crammed full of interesting information. A fantastic holiday and my best ever learning experience. — *no it wasn't!*

Doug Freeburn, Sydney, Australia.

Not only did Giovanni, our guide, bring history to life with his fascinating stories and facts, but he also took us to some wonderful restaurants, where we ate like kings at very low prices. It was a real cultural feast! Mille grazie. — *wish I could say the same – very pricey*

Susana and Reiner Enkelmann, Filderstadt, Germany

And as you know, I'm off to Rome with Timson's Tours next month. It's a shame I couldn't book the same dates as you – it would have been nice to go with someone I know. But at least now you can tell me how you got on. Was it really as good as all those people make it out to be in their testimonials on the website? Did you have a good guide?

Let me know if there's anything I should know before I go. 'Forewarned is forearmed', as they say – this is the first time I've been abroad for ages and I'd like to go as prepared as possible.

2   **A** and **B** below are the first half of the two letters required by the task. Use the underlined information in **A**, the informal letter, to complete the gaps in **B**, the formal letter. Write **one** word in each gap. There is an example at the beginning (0).

A

Dear Sarah

Just <u>got back</u> from Rome and found your letter waiting for me. <u>I had a very good week</u> there – the guide, Francesca, really made it for me and I learnt <u>loads</u> about the history of Rome. She really <u>knew</u> her subject and she <u>explained</u> things so well.

The website testimonials are fairly accurate, but I've just written to Timson's to <u>tell</u> them about two or three things that happened when I was there. It's really a way of helping them to <u>make things better</u> for future tours – like the one you're going on next month!

<u>For one thing</u>, we never made it to Ostia because the coach broke down shortly after we <u>left</u> and the local rep <u>didn't send</u> another one to replace it. <u>Also</u>, we had three free days rather than two, because our guide suddenly fell <u>ill</u> at the end and we were left to look after ourselves. <u>One last thing</u> that'll be of particular interest to you – I only <u>found out</u> when I <u>got to</u> Rome that we had to pay to <u>get into</u> all the ancient monuments ourselves, which I thought was a bit cheeky considering the price.

That last point is certainly something for you to bear in mind when you go – make sure you …

B

Dear Sir or Madam

I have just (0) <u>returned</u> from Rome, where I spent a week on one of your historical tours. I would like to express my general (1) _____ with the holiday, during which I learnt a great (2) _____ about Rome and its history. This was largely due to the excellent work of the guide, Francesca, who impressed everyone with her (3) _____ and the quality of her (4) _____ .

I feel I should, however, draw your (5) _____ to a number of incidents which occurred, in the hope that this may help you to (6) _____ your service in future. (7) _____, our planned visit to Ostia was cancelled, as the bus broke down soon after our (8) _____ and your local representative (9) _____ to send a replacement. In (10) _____, our two free days became three, owing to the unexpected (11) _____ of our guide on the final day; once again, we were not provided with a substitute. (12) _____ , I was rather surprised to (13) _____ on my (14) _____ in Rome that (15) _____ fees to ancient monuments were not included in the price of the holiday.

As a result of my experience, I would like to make a number of recommendations for future tours.

3   Now complete each of the letters, using the following plans as a guide. You should write **100–125 words for each letter**.

A Giving advice to your friend
- costs of admission – take enough money
- guidebook poor – buy your own
- restaurants can be pricey – check in guidebook/ask guide about cheap ones

B Making recommendations to Timson's
- arrange alternative if bus breaks down, guide sick etc.
- make ad more explicit, eg admission costs
- improve guidebook (say how)

Don't forget!
- Continue each letter using the same informal or formal register.
- End each letter in an appropriate way.
- Use a wide range of language.

What to expect in the exam
- In Part 1 of the Writing Paper you may have to write more than one task type.
- The overall word limit for Part 1 Writing tasks is approximately **250** words.

Reading

Gapped text

For questions **1–6**, choose which of the paragraphs **A–G** on page 21 fit into the gaps in the following magazine article. There is one extra paragraph which does not fit in any of the gaps.

> **Don't forget!**
>
> Read through the whole of the base text (the main text with the gaps) before you start to make your choices.

The house of maps

The world of geography owes a big debt to Stanfords, suppliers of maps to the world. As the company celebrates its 150th anniversary this month, Peter Whitfield traces the company's early history.

During the winter of 1887, John Ruskin, art critic, moralist and sage, dashed off a cry for help to a well known London shop: *Gentlemen, have you any school atlas on sale at present without railroads in its maps? Of all the entirely odd stupidities of modern education, railroads in maps are infinitely the oddest to my mind. Ever your faithful servant and victim, J Ruskin.* The recipient of this rather strange appeal was the firm of Edward Stanford, the map-seller who had made himself pre-eminent in his field.

1 _____

The first Edward Stanford launched his business in 1853 when he took over the map shop of Trelawney Saunders in Charing Cross, London. He had left school at 14 to learn printing, moving on to work in a number of shops before joining Saunders in the map trade. Of course there were trade rivals but what put them ahead was Stanford's recognition that the 19th century was experiencing a rising demand for maps of all kinds.

2 _____

Of the personality of the first Edward Stanford we know little, but his son, the second Edward Stanford who became head of the firm in 1882, emerges more clearly, thanks to the survival of both business and personal papers. A formidable autocrat, he ruled his house with an iron grip for 35 years. In his business letters he made it clear that *Stanfords* was no mere shop, but a service for gentlemen governed by gentlemen. His correspondents included some of the outstanding geographers of the age, many of whom commissioned *Stanfords* to carry out cartographic work for them.

3 _____

It was under this man's direction that the firm's publishing programme reached its high-point with *Stanford's London Atlas of Universal Geography*, a massive folio atlas first issued in 1887, containing almost 100 detailed maps and reprinted several times. As a textual companion to the atlas, the firm also published the magnificent *Stanford's Compendium of Geography and Travel*, a six-volume encyclopaedia of geography written by a team of first-class scholars; a new edition appeared in the 1890s, giving two volumes to each continent.

4 _____

This could only be of benefit to sales and the rewards were substantial. Stanford prospered, the business was entirely his own and he spent its profits freely. He sent his three sons to Oxford University, bought a large villa in a London suburb and a country house on the coast. He took his holidays abroad and invested in the stock exchange. This prosperity was a world away from the lowly tradesman's upbringing his father had known in the 1830s. A reversal of fortune, however, was soon to come.

5

In the event, all three sons survived and Edward Fraser Stanton returned from the Middle East to become director of the business. But a historical and social chasm had opened up between the pre-war world and the 1920s. The family's earlier prosperity, a university education and the army had transformed the mental horizons of the Stanford children: they lost their enthusiasm for trade and became officers and gentlemen.

6

This freed *Stanfords* to concentrate on retailing and, finally, to take advantage of the revolution in travel that began to gather pace in the late 1960s. The package tourist heading for the beaches has little use for maps, but for the independent and discerning traveller, maps are essential companions. By importing maps from the four corners of the globe, *Stanfords* has maintained its unique role as a fountainhead of mapping and travel literature, even though this material is no longer published by *Stanfords* itself.

A The colonial administrator, the railway or mining engineer, the newspaper editor and the tourist all required maps, and within a few short years of his appointment at the shop, Stanford had initiated a map-publishing programme that would become the most comprehensive in England. After securing agencies for the sale of official maps produced by overseas and colonial survey authorities, he set about reducing this detailed survey information into smaller-scale accurate and up-to-date maps.

B In contrast to his dealings with these figures, there were the day-to-day skirmishes with insolent customers, resentful trade rivals and tedious officials. Stanford hears himself verbally abused when he asks for payments almost a year overdue, and he curtly reminds another offended customer that 'truth is apt to be considered discourtesy' when it refers to painful matters such as unpaid debts.

C Alongside these achievements, the Stanford name was synonymous with the maps of Ordnance Survey but they also acted as sales agent for many other official bodies, including *The Royal Geographical Society* and the War Office. Its role as distributor of these official survey maps gave the business a unique status, reinforcing the perception that its own maps must be authoritative and accurate.

D Consequently, some vital energy seemed to desert the business: the golden age of *Stanfords'* map-publishing was over, and the firm was ill-equipped to survive the years of economic depression ahead. The struggling business was eventually sold to George Philip and all *Stanfords'* cartographic activities were absorbed into those of the parent company.

E Whether you sought an Ordnance Survey map of an English county, a map of a European war-zone, of the railways of India or the goldfields of South Africa, such a reputation meant that *Stanfords* was always the first port of call. This year, *Stanfords* is celebrating a century and a half of map-selling, during which time the company has had a small but intriguing role in Britain's political and social history.

F The First World War was to all but eliminate the firm. Many of its staff enlisted or were conscripted; private foreign travel virtually halted overnight; and all three of Stanford's sons were commissioned as junior officers. The effect was catastrophic and the strain on the ageing 'governor' proved fatal: when he died the firm was deep in debt and its future looked dark.

G This was a risk that Stanford was willing to take. Their property was rebuilt and reopened at Covent Garden with a splendid new showroom and space for all the cartographical and printing work on the floors above.

Vocabulary

Wordlist on page 210 of the Coursebook.

Adjective and noun collocations

1 Complete the crossword using the clues below. Each of the answers is a noun which collocates with the adjective in bold. All the collocations have appeared in units **1–3** of the Coursebook.

Across

3 He hopes to fulfil his **burning** _____ to become world champion.

5 The kitchen was filled with the **delightful** _____ of freshly baked bread.

6 Mailshots have proved to be the most **cost effective** _____ of marketing our products.

8 The organizers claim that the demonstration was 'a **resounding** _____'.

11 It made a **welcome** _____ to win – I was getting tired of losing.

12 She now faces the **daunting** _____ of writing a successful sequel to her hugely popular first book.

Down

1 The Prime Minister yesterday announced **sweeping** _____ to her Cabinet.

2 He could smell the **pungent** _____ of rotten eggs.

4 The newspaper has been accused of publishing **misleading** _____ in relation to the case.

7 The government claims that the demonstration was 'a **dismal** _____'.

9 We still have an **outside** _____ of qualifying for the finals.

10 The pile of old clothes gave off a damp, **musty** _____ .

2 For each noun you wrote in exercise 1, write two further adjectives which collocate with it.

Verb and noun collocations

1 Match each of the nouns in the box to one of the groups of verbs **1–8**. All the verbs in the group must collocate with the noun. The first one has been done for you.

information	change	a problem	a possibility
a challenge	~~success~~	an ambition	a smell

1 achieve	deserve	enjoy	meet with	_success_
2 achieve	fulfil	pursue	realize	_____
3 broadcast	gather	provide	publish	_____
4 face	present	rise to	take up	_____
5 bring about	call for	cope with	resist	_____
6 come up against	face up to	resolve	run into	_____
7 ignore	look into	overlook	rule out	_____
8 detect	get rid of	give off	leave	_____

2   Complete each of the gaps with the appropriate form of a verb from exercise 1. The first one has been done for you.

1   He was a brilliant musician, who thoroughly *deserved* the **success** he had – though I don't think it made him any happier.

2   She still finds time to _____ her **ambition** to become a professional opera singer, though she is aware she may never achieve it.

3   I've been _____ **information** on minority languages for my next book.

4   The recent dramatic increase in the number of burglaries _____ a major **challenge** to the police.

5   The only way to progress is by welcoming **change**, not _____ it.

6   The company faced a number of **problems**, most of which it has now tackled and successfully _____ .

7   We're currently _____ the **possibility** of opening new premises; it depends on the company's performance over the next year.

8   It stinks of smoke in here! Could you open the window to _____ the **smell**?

Word formation

Complete each gap with an appropriate form of the word in capitals at the end of the line. There is an example at the beginning (0).

> ### Don't forget!
> You may need to use the negative form of an adjective or adverb.

0   As a student, I'm still *financially* dependent on my parents.   **FINANCE**

1   Unfortunately, many people are still worryingly _____ of the facts about AIDS.   **IGNORE**

2   There are _____ versions of Vivaldi's *Four Seasons*, but this recording is by far the best I've heard.   **COUNT**

3   We'll have to walk to the village – it's _____ to cars.   **ACCESS**

4   We have discussed these problems on _____ occasions and still nothing has been decided.   **NUMBER**

5   Not _____ perhaps, sales of air conditioning systems increased considerably during the recent hot spell.   **SURPRISE**

6   *Bed of Roses*, widely seen as the finest _____ work about the period, was published in 1976.   **LITERATE**

7   After several _____ attempts, he finally passed his driving test in June last year.   **SUCCEED**

8   A _____ study of farming procedures in fifteen African countries has just been published.   **COMPARE**

9   Unemployment rose _____ last year.   **DRAMA**

10 As a special _____ offer, there is a 10% discount on all kitchen units in the new range.   **INTRODUCE**

Language focus

 Grammar reference on page 217 of the Coursebook.

1 Complete each of the gaps with **two** words. Contractions (eg haven't, don't etc) count as two words. There is an example at the beginning (0).

0 She went on holiday with her friends, though we'd rather _she had_ come with us.

1 It was a terrible film. I wish we _____ the French one instead.

2 She found out from Jerry, but I'd _____ told her myself.

3 If it hadn't _____ Eleanor's excellent negotiation skills, we might never have reached an agreement.

4 I should _____ my gloves – my hands were freezing.

5 Most employees would prefer _____ been given a bonus rather than an expensive Christmas hamper.

6 _____ known he intended to resign, I'd never have sacked him.

7 If only _____ spoken to me about it before; I _____ done something to help you.

8 The accident _____ have happened if he hadn't _____ at 90 miles an hour.

2 Tick (✔) those endings which can complete the sentences. Either one, two or all three answers are possible.

1 I'd much rather
  A you have told me the truth.
  B I have a motorbike than a car.
  C have gone shopping on my own.

2 If she didn't want to see you,
  A she wouldn't have invited you to her party.
  B what would you do?
  C she used to get me to tell you she wasn't at home.

3 If it hadn't been for the rain,
  A we didn't get wet.
  B we could have eaten outside.
  C we've enjoyed ourselves very much.

4 I couldn't have done it financially
  A if my parents hadn't supported me.
  B had it not been for the financial support of my parents.
  C without the financial support of my parents.

5 If you push that button,
  A it goes faster.
  B you'll regret it.
  C nothing would happen.

6 I wish I
  A would have more time to do everything.
  B had had more time to do everything.
  C had more time to do everything.

7 If I were to lend him the money,
  A he hadn't paid it back.
  B he wouldn't have paid it back.
  C he'd have to pay it back soon.

8 I'll tell her what you think
  A if I happen to see her.
  B should she be interested?
  C if that's alright with you.

English in Use

Multiple-choice cloze

For questions **1–15**, read the text below and then decide which answer **A, B, C** or **D** best fits each space. The exercise begins with an example **(0)**.

> **Don't forget!**
> Read the text through first before you start to make your choices.

Garbology

To most people, landfill sites are **(0)** _____ holes in the ground where waste **(1)** _____ is buried. To garbologists, however, they provide a valuable **(2)** _____ of information about a population's activities in **(3)** _____ such as food consumption and waste disposal. Garbology is a branch of ethnography, a science which abandons traditional methods of **(4)** _____ market research information, such as questionnaires and focus groups, in favour of **(5)** _____ observation of people and their habits.

The world's **(6)** _____ garbologist, Professor William Rathje, is also an archaeologist. Archaeologists study past cultures by examining the **(7)** _____ of objects and buildings, but the basic principles of archaeology can also be **(8)** _____ to the discarded rubbish of present-day civilizations in order to **(9)** _____ a better understanding of how people behave now. As founder and director of the Garbage Project at the University of Arizona, Professor Rathje has **(10)** _____ over 30 years of his life to the archaeological study of modern refuse.

His work is of **(11)** _____ interest to commerce; companies need to understand the lives of their consumers in order to create brands which will be of most **(12)** _____ to them. Rathje's **(13)** _____ can help them achieve this. In addition, his analysis of the composition of landfill sites reveals a greater need not only to recycle more rubbish, but also to **(14)** _____ down on the amount of rubbish we produce in the first **(15)** _____ .

	A	**B**	**C**	**D**
0	easily	<u>simply</u>	bluntly	directly
1	selection	product	fabric	material
2	spring	origin	source	fountain
3	areas	regions	locations	parts
4	holding	meeting	obtaining	comprising
5	near	close	tight	hard
6	heading	leading	charging	fronting
7	rests	ruins	relics	remains
8	employed	attributed	attached	applied
9	gain	learn	make	gather
10	conveyed	devoted	apportioned	spent
11	high	large	great	deep
12	function	serving	use	purpose
13	outcomes	findings	implications	derivations
14	lower	cut	bring	get
15	place	situation	way	time

Writing

CAE Part 1

Formal letters

1 Read the following Writing Part 1 task. Before you write your answer, do the related tasks in **A–C** on page 27.

You are studying at a college in the Parkdale area of Blatchington in England. You have read an article in the local newspaper about a proposal to close the local library, which is opposite your college. As a result of the article, your class conducted interviews and did a survey among Parkdale residents. You have decided to write a letter to the editor of the newspaper, responding to the article, briefly summarizing the information from the survey and explaining why you feel the library should not be closed.

Read the newspaper article, on which you have made some notes, together with the survey results and the comments from Parkdale residents. Then, **using the information carefully**, write your **letter** to the newspaper editor (approximately **250** words).

You should use your own words as far as possible.

'Library should close,' says councillor

LOCAL COUNCILLOR David Markham has called for the closure of the public library in the Parkdale area of Blatchington. According to Mr Markham the Parkdale library is underused, with most residents preferring the much larger Central Library in Green Street. "Over the years a great deal of money has been injected into the Parkdale library," explained Councillor Markham, "yet local residents have failed to take advantage of the facilities. The building could be converted into a sports facility to make it pay its way."

This newspaper can confirm that Parkdale residents do indeed seem to have abandoned their local library. Reporters visiting the library on three successive mornings found no more than a handful of people using the facilities on each occasion.

not everyone can get there easily

more important to have a decent library

where's the proof?

nonsense!

when fewest people go

Class survey of Parkdale residents

How often do you use the Parkdale library?		When do you go there? (Percentage of those using the library)	
At least three times a week	9%	Mornings (9am–1pm)	17%
Once or twice a week	38%	Afternoons (1pm–6pm)	36%
About once a month	41%	Evenings (6pm–9pm)	47%
Never	12%		

Typical comments from Parkdale residents

1 If the facilities were better, more people might use the library. They could begin by buying some more recent novels – the ones they've got are pretty old and in very poor condition.

2 We don't need any more sports facilities in Parkdale – we've already got the sports centre and the swimming pool.

3 I read the newspapers there every morning. I'm a disabled pensioner and the main library in Green Street is just too far for me to travel to every day.

4 It's the only place where I can study in the evening – it's too noisy at home. They could do with some more reference books, though, or even better, some computers with access to the Internet.

A Organizing the information in the input material

In Writing Part 1 tasks, it is sometimes possible to find connections between different parts of the input material. For each of the handwritten notes on the newspaper article, find one or more corresponding pieces of information in the survey results and/or typical comments. The first one has been done for you.

1 not everyone can get there easily   *Comment 3 – pensioner*

2 where's the proof?   _____

3 more important to have a decent library _____

4 nonsense!   _____

5 when fewest people go   _____

B Summarizing the information in the survey

Which of the following sentences would be more appropriate for your letter? Why?

1 *In our survey 9% of the people we interviewed use the Parkdale library at least three times a week, 38% use it once or twice a week, 41% go there about once a month and only 12% never use it.*

2 *Almost half of those residents interviewed visit the library at least once a week and only a relatively small percentage said they make no use of its facilities at all.*

C Using your own words

Where possible you should avoid copying the language contained in the input material. Complete each of the gaps in sentences **1–5** with one of the nouns from the box. Then match each sentence to the handwritten note on the newspaper article which it expresses.

journey	claim	period	evidence	priority

1 This is the least busy _____ of the day.

2 _____ should be given to the improvement of the existing service.

3 Some residents are unable to make the _____ into the town centre.

4 Your _____ that local residents do not use the library is untrue.

5 There is little _____ of this investment.

2 Now write your answer to the task in approximately **250** words.

Don't forget!

Your letter should be consistently formal throughout.
Look again at pages 23 and 196 of the Coursebook for information on writing Part 1 Formal letters.

4 Work time

CAE Part 3 · Multiple choice

Read the following magazine article about work and holidays. Answer questions **1–7** by choosing a letter **A, B, C** or **D**. Give only one answer to each question.

No cure for the summertime blues

Paul Gould looks at the highs of going away and the lows as your post-holiday glow fades.

Irrespective of the destination; it's the coming back that hurts. As you trudge in to work and the old routine, post-holiday blues hit whether you've been to Barbados or Benidorm. I once had them after a week in hardly-exotic Wolverhampton. It is a recognized psychological pattern: we switch to a low after a high, we get despondent when a spell of basking in bliss is abruptly ended.

For me, that bliss was tasted at its most intoxicating two years ago in a secluded bay in southern Crete. At the time, a fortnight seemed to expand into a way of life. Days were taken up with massage, sunbathing, swimming and yoga. There was constant camaraderie and laughter. Being a wage-slave seemed inconceivable: I was born to dance and sing, chill out and be pampered. This, I felt, was how life should be. More unsettling, though, was my conviction that life could be like this. If only I could cling on to this happy state, open to the blessings of life, my potential for joy and creativity would be unlocked.

It couldn't last. The blues set in even before the holiday ended. What we needed, one of our group declared over prolonged farewell drinks at the taverna, was a post-holiday trauma support group. Is trauma too strong a word? Cary Cooper, professor of psychology at the University of Manchester, says the symptoms are undoubtedly genuine: "It's things like being more aggressive or more withdrawn, mild depression, feeling tired even after a good night's sleep. Really, you're angry at the lifestyle you're re-entering but you can't take it out on your lifestyle so you take it out on other people."

So what of my hope of clinging on to that holiday feeling? My resolutions were to continue yoga classes, to take up massage and to rise above stress. Couldn't I maintain that way of life? "The reason you don't is that people get really absorbed in work, then get on the train or whatever, and by the time they get home they're exhausted and just flop in front of the TV," says Professor Cooper. The post-holiday glow may last a day or two. There's the gratification of colleagues asking where you've been. It can be quite amusing for the first morning when there's plenty of show-off mileage in telling people you've been to exciting places having more fun than them. But then day-to-day hassles crowd in thick and fast. The holiday may well have seemed like ages at the time, but now it shrinks to a tiny blip. You feel cheated.

Perhaps holidays give us an unrealistic taste of fantasy. I detect something altogether darker: they compel us to see how much aggravation, tedium and mediocrity we put up with the rest of the time. On a more paranoid note, is it possible we've been intoxicated by a cynical holidays industry? Are holidays just a mechanism whereby we swap our role as producers in the great big economic machine for that of the consumer? Professor Cooper confirms my fears: "We go on holiday and become consumers and because work is so time-consuming, the way we justify it is to use the money to make us feel better about our limited existence, saying: 'At least I can afford a nice holiday.'" Surely we can't just blame the industry? Some of my best holidays have simply been times when I chose to hang out with friends, have long conversations, feel carefree. Such was that week in Wolverhampton – on which, Professor Cooper's verdict was: "It was about investing in relationships."

After a holiday, Professor Cooper advises going back to work gradually: "Do only the stuff that needs immediate attention, leave on time, go to the gym." Thank goodness work-life balance has entered public debate. It is high time we got agitated about the realisation that four weeks' holiday a year and a working week of 40 hours plus means we can set aside no time or energy for things that matter, such as our partners, our children, our friends, staying healthy, or cooking instead of ready meals. But Professor Cooper's advice so far is mere tinkering at the edges. A more revolutionary solution is downshifting. "People see the gap between a normal human life and the treadmill existence and realize the cost is too great," he says. "So they think: 'Why not work for a smaller company or set up on my own?'"

Yet the long-hours culture is probably only part of the problem. That post-exotica malaise is also brought on by sheer boredom, noisy neighbours or, worse, domestic discord. The traditional saying is "There's no place like home" but it sometimes seems there's no place like away from it all. In his acclaimed book *The Art of Travel*, Alain de Botton sums up this yearning: "Few seconds in life are more releasing than those in which a plane ascends to the sky … its ascent is a symbol of transformation. It can inspire us to imagine analogous, decisive shifts in our own lives; to imagine that we too might one day surge above much that looms over us." So perhaps the only way to cure post-holiday blues is to start planning the next one as soon as you get back.

1 In the first paragraph, the writer suggests that post-holiday feelings of depression

   A occur when a holiday has been cut short.
   B happen regardless of the holiday destination.
   C arise when a holiday has not been satisfying.
   D affect people more whose jobs are routine.

2 During his holiday in Crete, the writer was

   A resentful about an illusion of happiness.
   B certain he could maintain that way of living.
   C determined to start working for himself.
   D astonished at the change in his behaviour.

3 What does Professor Cary Cooper believe about trauma?

   A People have a tendency to confuse stress with trauma.
   B It has a serious impact on performance at work.
   C Holidays can only increase trauma which already exists in a person.
   D It can cause people to behave in an unpleasant way towards others.

4 What are we told about people who have been back at work for a few days?

   A They feel as though the holiday they had was too short.
   B They exaggerate when describing it to their colleagues.
   C They lack the mental discipline to maintain a lifestyle change.
   D They underestimate the time they need to commit to work.

5 In the fifth paragraph, the writer states that going on holiday forces people to

   A focus on relationships they have neglected.
   B be keener to assert their superior social status.
   C recognize the frustrations of everyday life.
   D work longer hours in order to afford time off.

6 In the sixth paragraph, one of the writer's aims is to

   A encourage people to protest about their working hours.
   B persuade people of the value of personal relationships.
   C highlight which of Professor Cooper's proposals are valid.
   D illustrate the advantages of people becoming self-employed.

7 The writer's purpose in using the quotation from *The Art of Travel* is to

   A contrast people's dreams with what they actually go on to achieve.
   B promote the idea that risk-takers lead a more rewarding life.
   C discourage people from settling down before they are ready.
   D show the pleasure derived from dreaming about a different lifestyle.

Vocabulary

Wordlist on page 211 of the Coursebook.

A Adjectives of personality

Match each of the adjectives to an appropriate description.

slapdash	approachable	attentive	trustworthy
industrious	domineering	single-minded	conceited

1 She always works very hard. _____

2 He doesn't take much care over his work. _____

3 She's so friendly and easy to talk to. _____

4 He thinks he's so intelligent – it's extremely irritating. _____

5 The staff are always so polite and helpful. _____

6 Her only aim is to become managing director. _____

7 Your secret is safe with her. _____

8 He tries to control others without any consideration
for their feelings or opinions. _____

B Time

Complete each of the gaps with one of the words from the box.

at	aside	for	of	in
to	out	on	off	up

1 Sorry, I can't stop to chat – I'm a little **pressed _____ time**.

2 We had hoped to discuss the matter in the meeting but we **ran _____ of time**.

3 I always try to **set _____ some time** each day to read the newspaper.

4 We have a huge garden, which **takes _____ most of my free time**.

5 Not many people have heard of her, but **it's only a matter _____ time before**
she becomes famous.

6 I did as much as I could _____ **the time available**.

7 We didn't arrange to meet _____ **any specific time**, but I'm surprised he's not
here yet.

8 He is retiring from his post in order to **devote more time _____ his family**.

9 She always gets straight to the point; she doesn't like to **waste time _____**
small talk.

10 All pregnant women in this country have the right to **take time _____ work** for
antenatal care.

Self help

Add the expressions in bold in B to your vocabulary notebook.

C Skills

Complete the crossword by solving the anagrams. Each answer is a single-word item of vocabulary which collocates with the word **skills**. The first one has been done for you.

Across
- **4** mop truce
- **8** lice chant
- **10** comic mountain
- **11** rose plan

Down
- **1** pen to heel
- **2** an ailing rat zoo
- **3** arctic pal
- **5** busses in
- **6** a secret rail
- **7** a mail range
- **9** a lung age

Language focus

 Grammar reference on page 219 of the Coursebook.

Gerunds and infinitives

Complete the second sentence so that it has a similar meaning to the first sentence. Use the word given, without changing it in any way. There is an example at the beginning **(0)**.

0 She will often panic if there is a problem.
tendency
She _has a tendency to panic if there is a problem._

1 I was surprised when he said he wouldn't work overtime.
refusal
His _____

2 Don't bother to read that book.
worth
It _____

3 Shall I carry your bag for you?
like
Would _____

4 He tried very hard to give up smoking.
effort
He _____

5 I'm very grateful to you for coming at such short notice.
appreciate
I really _____

6 I found it impossible not to laugh when he said that.
help
I _____

7 If you don't leave now, you'll miss the bus.
better
You _____

8 I find it difficult to remember names.
difficulty
I _____

9 They made us clean up the mess.
made
We _____

10 She didn't like the fact that he had been treated so badly.
being
She objected _____

English in Use

CAE Part 2

Open cloze

For questions **1–15**, complete the following article by writing **one** word in each space. The exercise begins with an example **(0)**.

Don't forget!

- Read the text through first before you start to make your choices.
- The emphasis is on grammatical words, such as prepositions, auxiliary verbs and articles.

Female butlers

A new breed of butlers has appeared **(0)** _on_ the scene; increasingly, it seems **(1)** _____ rich and famous are turning **(2)** _____ women to perform the little domestic duties of everyday life. But **(3)** _____ female butlers are in ever greater demand, they are also in short supply. Ivor Spencer, who runs the **(4)** _____ traditional of the well known butler schools, **(5)** _____ trained only eight women in 21 years. Even at the more progressive butler academies, **(6)** _____ as Robert Watson's Guild of Professional Butlers, fewer than one **(7)** _____ four trainees are female.

Butlerine Sarah Whittle says that women are in demand **(8)** _____ they're less stuffy than men. "We're better **(9)** _____ picking up on people's moods," she says. "And we can organize several things at **(10)** _____ : it's in our nature to multitask." Whittle **(11)** _____ expected to be smart and professional **(12)** _____ duty, but she does get glamorous perks – presents of chocolate, champagne and, on **(13)** _____ occasion, an expensive pair of shoes. But the job has its downside. Hundred-hour weeks are **(14)** _____ uncommon, the hours are unsociable and the tasks often **(15)** _____ than glamorous.

CAE Part 4   **Word formation**

For questions **1–15**, use the words in the boxes to the right of the texts to form **one** word that fits the same numbered space in the text. The exercise begins with an example **(0)**.

Sales manager

As part of its major new programme of **(0)** *expansion,* RAL Cosmetics is seeking to appoint a dynamic sales professional to run a team of sales **(1)** _____ in the UK. You will be highly-motivated, with the drive and determination to be the best in your field. You will also have strong **(2)** _____ qualities and be an effective **(3)** _____ . The position will involve frequent travel to Europe for **(4)** _____ at international sales conferences and training courses at our head office in Lyon. Previous experience in the cosmetics industry is **(5)** _____ though not essential. We guarantee a **(6)** _____ remuneration package, including a company car and a contributory pension scheme.

If you feel you have the necessary qualities and background, send your CV to Alain Sylvestre, 22 rue Marivaux, 69142 Lyon, France.

(7) _____ date for applications: September 25th

0	EXPAND
1	REPRESENT
2	LEAD
3	COMMUNICATE
4	ATTEND
5	PREFER
6	COMPETE
7	CLOSE

Stress

The term 'stress' is frequently given as the **(8)** _____ for a range of minor complaints and conditions **(9)** _____ from the frantic pace of modern life. A work colleague's bad temper, for example, or our own splitting headache, might be put down to stress. Stress is not the same as pressure. Pressure is stimulating and energizing; stress arises from our **(10)** _____ to cope with that pressure and can have **(11)** _____ consequences for our health. Researchers have identified a number of symptoms (see below) which often occur before more serious stress-related illnesses take over.

Some physical symptoms
- A lack of appetite
- Frequent indigestion or heartburn
- Insomnia
- A **(12)** _____ to sweat for no reason

Some (13) _____ **symptoms**
- Irritability
- Difficulty **(14)** _____
- Loss of sense of humour
- Constant **(15)** _____

8	EXPLAIN
9	RESULT
10	ABLE
11	HARM
12	TEND
13	BEHAVIOUR
14	CONCENTRATE
15	TIRED

Writing

Reports

1 Read the following Writing Part 2 task.

An international research group is carrying out an investigation into changing trends in the way young people spend their free time. You have been asked to write a report about the situation in your country. You should:

- describe the changes that have taken place over the last twenty years in the way that young people spend their free time
- say whether these changes have been for the better or the worse
- suggest how you think the situation might develop in the future.

Write your **report** in approximately **250** words.

2 The following report was written in answer to the task above by a British person **in the mid-nineteen sixties**. Put the paragraphs in the correct order, using the underlined words to help you. Then write a suitable heading for each paragraph.

Young people's leisure time activities

1 ....

The growth in popularity of the car has made once popular pastimes rather dangerous. Street games such as football, skipping or marbles are no longer such a common sight. Similarly, cycling on the open road is becoming less attractive, particularly with the construction of motorways, which began at the end of the last decade. Sadly, youngsters now spend more time in the home, where another invention has radically transformed their habits.

2 ....

The main difference between now and twenty years ago is the increased wealth and greater amount of free time available to young people. This, in itself, represents a welcome change, but two other developments have restricted the nature and quality of leisure time activities.

3 ....

It is highly likely that television will continue to dominate the lives of our youth in the years to come. Teenagers and people in their twenties may well spend most of their spare time at home, simply watching TV programmes or listening to their latest long-playing records. They might even begin to wish they had less free time on their hands.

4 ....

The purpose of this report is to comment on recent changes in the way young people make use of their spare time in my country and to consider possible future trends.

5 ....

Where previously whole families would gather round the radio to listen to a gripping drama, now children fight with their parents over which of the two television channels they should select. Courting couples rarely go ballroom dancing or join long queues outside cinemas and music halls as they once did; instead, they stay in to watch television or perhaps worse, attend wild pop concerts or parties, where they dance in uncontrolled ways.

---

3 Find examples in the model of the following:

Language used to compare the past and the present	Different ways of referring to young people
eg *once popular pastimes*	eg *youngsters*

Language used to make future predictions	Different ways of referring to free time
eg *It is highly likely that television will continue …*	

4 Underline those words and expressions which express the writer's opinion on whether the changes have been for the better or the worse.

   eg *This, in itself, represents a welcome change …*

5 The writer of the report uses a consistently formal register. Sometimes, this involves using nouns rather than verbs. For each of the following, find the equivalent expression in the model answer.

   a The car has become more and more popular …

   _____

   b … especially because they've built motorways …

   _____

   c … young people have more money and more free time.

   _____

6 Now write your own answer to the question on page 34.

Useful language

Refer to the following sections in the Wordlist of the Coursebook:
● Possibility: page 210
● Change: page 210

Don't forget!

● Plan your answer before you write.
● Use a consistently formal register.
● Link one paragraph with the next, as in the model.
● Give your report a title and each of your paragraphs a heading.

Reading

Multiple choice

Read the following newspaper article about the effect that different types of technology have on people's emotions. Answer questions **1–6** by choosing a letter **A, B, C** or **D**. Give only one answer to each question.

Machine rage is dead ... long live emotional computing

You have spent the last 20 minutes talking to an automated call centre. A passionless, computerized voice drones out assurances and urges you to press yet another key. Your blood pressure soars. Finally you hurl your phone at the wall. Or your teenage son becomes immersed, with increasing agitation, in a computer game. As his temper worsens, his performance declines until he ends up trashing the console in a fit of adolescent rage. Computer angst – now a universal feature of modern life – is an expensive business when you come to think of it!

Fortunately, the days of the unfeeling machine will soon be over. Thanks to breakthroughs in artificial intelligence, psychology, electronics and other research fields, scientists are now creating computers and robots that can detect, and respond to, users' feelings. The discoveries are being channelled by *Humaine*, a £6 million programme that has just been launched by the European Union to give Europe a lead in emotional computing. As a result, computers will soon detect our growing irritation at their behaviour and in turn generate more sympathetic, human-like messages or slow down the tempo of the games they are running. Robots will be able to react in lifelike ways, though we may end up releasing some unwelcome creations too. 'Computers that can detect and imitate human emotion may sound like science fiction, but they are already with us,' said Dr Dylan Evans, a key *Humaine* project collaborator.

Recent developments include the launch of *Face Station* software that can determine human emotions from webcam images; the creation of humanoid robots by scientists at Hertfordshire University which help autistic children to better understand and respond to other people's expressions and emotional states; and a virtual reality system created by Salford University scientists that is to be used as an anti-bullying teaching aid. All depend on scientists' new-found ability to recognize the physiological expressions of emotions – changes in stature, heart beat, muscle tension, head movement, rate and intensity of computer key strokes, blood pressure and other variables – and software that allows computers to recognize and respond to these variables.

'We give away our emotional state in all sorts of ways – we sigh, giggle nervously and speak at different rates,' said Dr Kate Cox of the school of psychology, at *Queen's University*, Belfast, where the *Humaine* project is being co-ordinated for the European Union. 'For example, when we get angry, our voice rises in pitch and volume. We tend to speak more quickly and our breathing gets faster. The muscles in our vocal cords tighten. Now we can quantify these, we can teach computers – and call centres – to recognize them. In the case of a call centre problem, a human operator could be channelled by the computer to break into the call, and stop the cycle of anger.'

At *Queen's Sonic Arts Research Centre*, scientists led by Professor Michael Alcorn are studying ways to detect the emotional states and reactions of computer game users – from the way they hold and tap on keyboards and consoles – so that machines can spot when feelings are beginning to run too high. 'The game could be slowed down and more soothing background music played,' said Alcorn. And a key breakthrough in the field of psychology has been the discovery that cool, unemotional decision-making, whether in game playing or for real, is seldom a desirable attribute. In fact, emotional involvement is a prerequisite for a sensible decision. 'The cold, unemotional character *Mr Spock* on the TV series *Star Trek* simply could not have evolved,' said artificial intelligence expert Professor Ruth Aylett of Salford University, another *Humaine* project leader.

Scientists are now anxious to learn how to replicate emotions so that they can build more effective, human-like robots, including humanoid devices that can aid the elderly. One such project has been launched by Dr Evans at the University of the West of England. He is using a robot dog which can recreate a range of canine emotions and behaviours, to see if the devices can provide companionship in residential homes. 'Of course, people say that just because you can teach a computer how to respond to a human does not mean you have made it emotionally sensitive,' said Evans. 'They say that you have merely taught it crude reaction techniques. But that is all that emotional sensitivity does for humans. It lets us spot people who are angry or aggressive or in some intense state and react accordingly. The sooner computers learn how to do that, the better it will be for them and us.'

1 What does the writer feel is the problem with modern technology?
  A It does not function in the intended way.
  B It causes friction between family members.
  C It can result in people losing their self-control.
  D It is impossible to achieve anything without technology.

2 What are we told about computers and robots in the second paragraph?
  A Computers will be able to adjust their behaviour to human need.
  B Robots may have superior social skills compared to some people.
  C Computers will be uniquely programmed to respond to individual users.
  D Europe has recently taken the lead in developments in technology.

3 What does the writer suggest about recent developments in the third paragraph?
  A They will only work once scientists have carried out further research.
  B They can be used to help people act more appropriately toward others.
  C The results are not yet consistent enough to be relied upon.
  D They are currently of little use for most people.

4 According to Dr Kate Cox, human emotion can
  A often be misinterpreted by other humans.
  B manifest itself differently in different people.
  C be accurately measured by scientists.
  D be dealt with effectively and entirely by computer.

5 The breakthrough in the field of psychology shows that
  A some people lack the ability to remain objective.
  B game players will not necessarily appreciate an easier game.
  C a degree of stress is necessary for people to perform well.
  D human emotion is a vital factor when making a choice.

6 How does Dr Dylan Evans defend the use of artificial intelligence?
  A He highlights cases where technological advances have helped people.
  B He mentions the machines that have already replaced human interaction.
  C He compares the reactions of a computer to those of humans.
  D He criticizes the ineffectiveness of some human social behaviour.

Vocabulary

Wordlist on page 211 of the Coursebook.

Adjective and noun collocations

1 Match each of the nouns in the box to one of the groups of adjectives **1–8**. All the adjectives in the group must collocate with the noun.

relationship					
argument					
love					
feelings	1 brotherly	first	true	unrequited	_____
family	2 inner	mixed	negative	strong	_____
friend	3 courting	elderly	married	young	_____
couple	4 close	love-hate	rocky	stable	_____
tension	5 best	close	mutual	school	_____
	6 adoptive	extended	immediate	single-parent	_____
	7 heated	furious	fierce	pointless	_____
	8 family	social	rising	heightened	_____

2 Complete each of the gaps with an appropriate adjective from exercise 1.

  1 I have a _____ **relationship** with my job; how I feel about it usually depends on what mood I'm in when I get to work.

  2 It was a _____ **argument**: neither of us was ever likely to change the other's way of thinking.

  3 Her latest novel is a tale of _____ **love**; Ross is besotted with his boss Hermione, who shows no interest in her young admirer.

  4 Sandra's parents have _____ **feelings** about her going to live abroad; they want her to lead her own life, but they'd be happier if she did so closer to home.

  5 We're not inviting any aunts or uncles and so on – just the _____ **family**.

  6 I met Paul on holiday and he's become quite a _____ **friend**.

Verbs

Complete each gap with the appropriate form of one of the verbs from the box. In each section **1–4**, the verb required for both spaces, **a** and **b**, is the same.

take	turn	call	fall

1 **a** The other children laughed at her, _____ **her names** and made her cry.
   b Alan Kelcher was very laid-back, and let his pupils _____ **him by his first name.**

2 **a** I always thought that love at first sight only happened in films, but I _____ **for** Jill the moment I set eyes on her.
   b She _____ **out with** her mother after a blazing row and hasn't spoken to her since.

3 **a** He had a friendly, open face and she _____ **an instant liking to** him.
   b In appearance she _____ **after** her father, but she's inherited her intelligence from her mother.

4 **a** He was heartbroken when she _____ **down** his proposal of marriage.
   b I usually _____ **to** my mother **for** help or advice: she's a better listener than my father.

Language focus

 Grammar reference on page 220 of the Coursebook.

Relative clauses

Correct the following sentences by changing the underlined word. You should write only **one** word.

1 We thought it was horrible, so we gave it to my mother, <u>she</u> loves that kind of thing.

2 The plane took off over two hours late, <u>what</u> meant I missed my connecting flight in Frankfurt.

3 He was criticized for giving a speech on a subject about <u>that</u> he knew very little.

4 There are two or three people in the photo <u>which</u> name I can't remember.

5 We're going back to the same hotel <u>that</u> we stayed last year.

6 I still don't understand the reason <u>because</u> they decided to close the sports centre.

7 My eldest son, <u>that</u> lives in Japan now, hardly ever comes back to visit us.

8 Kate and Steve were the only two people from work <u>to</u> came to our wedding.

Alternatives to relative clauses

1 Infinitives with 'to' can be used:
   • after words like *someone, nobody, anything* etc.
   *There is **nothing to suggest** that the crimes are connected.* (= nothing which suggests)
   • to replace relative clauses containing a modal verb.
   *There are **several dishes to choose from**.* (= several dishes which you can choose from)
   • after phrases like *the first, the next, the only* and superlatives.
   *The **next person to talk** will get extra homework.* (= next person who talks)
   *He has become the **oldest person ever to run** a marathon.* (= person who has ever run)

2 Relative clauses can be reduced by using:
   • a present participle
   ***Anyone wanting** further information, should contact Peter Wiley.* (= Anyone who wants)
   *Who's that **person sitting** next to your brother?* (= person who is sitting)
   • a past participle.
   *The two **men arrested** in connection with the robbery have been released without charge.* (= men who were/had been arrested)

1 Which famous siblings are described in each of the following pairs of sentences?

1 a They are not the only sisters ever to play each other in the final of a Wimbledon championship.
b Venus was champion in 2000 and 2001, but Serena was the one to collect the winner's trophy in 2002.

2 a When Michael was four, his father gave him a go-kart powered by a lawnmower engine.
b After a race, Ralf was usually the first to phone his mother.

3 a Some of their most famous films are *Monkey Business*, *Duck Soup* and *A Night at the Opera*, all released in the 1930s.
b One of the five brothers 'wore' a moustache painted on with black greasepaint; he found it easier than glueing one on.

4 a Fans hoping to see Janet in concert were disappointed to hear that she had cancelled her planned tour.
b Michael began his musical career at the age of five as the lead singer of a group comprising himself and four of his eight brothers and sisters.

5 a John was the youngest man ever to be elected President, and he was also the youngest to die.
b The biography does not make it clear whether Robert, known affectionately as Bobby, had evidence to back up his suspicions that the CIA had killed his brother.

2 Rewrite the underlined parts of the above sentences using relative pronouns.

Example: **1 a** the only sisters who have ever played each other

English in Use

CAE Part 3

Error correction

In **most** lines of the following text, there is **either** a spelling **or** a punctuation error. For each numbered line **1–16**, write the correctly spelled word or show the correct punctuation at the end of the line. Some lines are correct. Indicate these lines with a tick (✔). The exercise begins with three examples **(0)**, **(00)** and **(000)**.

How to marry rich

0	Ginie Sayles runs a relationship course in New York for men and	✔
00	women, hoping to marry into money. Julie Earle went along to one	*women hoping*
000	of her seminars to get some tips on how to find a wealthy spouce.	*spouse*
1	"The first rule," Ginie explains "is to live where the rich live. Change	
2	adress immediately if you're in the wrong area because research shows	
3	you'll marry someone with in sixteen blocks of where you live." If	
4	that means you can only afford a bedsit, dont worry. Wherever you're	
5	laying your head at night, you'll still be shopping in the right areas	
6	and sipping cappuccinos in the right cafés. All of this, will enable you	
7	to orchestrate a meeting with the right neighbour. Ginie also advises	
8	changing your name if you're unhappy with your currant one. "Cary	
9	Grant's real name was Archibald Leech," she tells me "When he	
10	changed it, he said he started to dress more elegantly and to be more	
11	elegant. If you choose a grate name, you tend to live up to it and have	
12	a stronger identity." Once you've moved house and swaped your name	
13	for something more exotique, you need to hang out at the playgrounds	
14	of the rich. "This means going to sport's events like polo, golf or high	
15	performance car racing. If you can't afford the entry ticket, get a job on	
16	the premises doing anything – even working behind the bar – will do."

CAE Part 5

Register transfer

For questions **1–13**, read the following letter from a form teacher and use the information in it to complete the numbered gaps in the letter to a friend. The words you need **do not occur** in the letter from the form teacher. **Use no more than two words in each gap**. The exercise begins with an example (**0**).

Letter from form teacher

Dear Mr and Mrs Wren

I am writing to express my <u>renewed</u> concern at the behaviour of your son, Michael. I have received a number of complaints relating to his conduct from several different teachers. These all make reference to the fact that he rarely pays attention in lessons and is constantly chatting with other pupils. As you will understand, this is a major source of irritation to teachers.

In addition, Michael has recently shown serious disrespect to the mathematics teacher, Ms Harding, to whom he spoke in an extremely offensive manner. This must not be allowed to reoccur. Finally, two days ago he was involved in yet another fight, this time with a boy who had insulted him. It would seem that Michael has still not mastered the art of keeping his temper under control in such situations.

Given the gravity of these complaints, I would like to invite you both to come to the school next Friday after school to discuss these matters with myself, in the hope of finding a solution.

Yours sincerely

Mrs Anne Robbins

4B Form Teacher

Letter to friend

Dear Rachel

Thanks for the letter. We're fine, except that Michael's in trouble at school (**0**) <u>again</u> . We've just had a letter from his form teacher, Mrs Robbins, saying how (**1**) _____ she is about the way he's been behaving at school. It seems quite (**2**) _____ of the teachers have complained about him. They all make the point that he hardly (**3**) _____ to what they're saying and he's (**4**) _____ chatting to his (**5**) _____ . I'm not surprised it (**6**) _____ their nerves!

He was also very (**7**) _____ to the maths teacher – I don't know what he said to her but I agree with Mrs Robbins that we mustn't let it (**8**) _____ again. Unfortunately, though, it doesn't (**9**) _____ there. Apparently, (**10**) _____ of days ago he got into a fight with someone who'd (**11**) _____ him names. It's not the first fight he's had, but I thought he'd learnt not (**12**) _____ his temper in situations like that.

We're going to the school next week to (**13**) _____ these things with Mrs Robbins to see if we can sort something out.

Writing

Character reference and note

1 Read the following Writing Part 1 task.

A friend of yours has applied for a job as a receptionist in a four-star hotel in Dublin. The personnel manager of the hotel has asked you to provide a character reference for your friend.

Read the job advertisement, the letters from the personnel manager and your friend, on which you have made some notes, and the list you have made of your friend's positive and negative qualities. Then, **using the information appropriately**, write:

a the **character reference** as requested by the personnel manager of the hotel (approximately 200 words);

b a brief **note** informing your friend that you have written the reference and wishing her luck with the application (approximately 50 words).

You should use your own words as far as possible.

Hotel Eire **** Receptionist

This prestigious four-star hotel on the outskirts of Dublin requires a dynamic receptionist with previous experience in a similar environment. He/She should be able to work as a member of a team, have excellent telephone and customer care skills and be able to remain calm under pressure. Applicants must also have a very high level of spoken and written English. Duties include checking customers in and out, handling customer accounts and close liaison with other employees in the hotel.

Contact James Hardcastle at jhardcas@hoteleire.ie

... I applied for that job in Dublin I told you about. I really hope I get it – it'd be great for my English and a brilliant opportunity for me to see Ireland. I'd even get to see my sister, who's studying at the University of Limerick. Anyway, I put your name down as a referee, so they might be in touch with you some time asking for a reference. Let me know if they do, because that might mean I get called for interview – assuming you write a good reference, of course!

already very good

definitely!

... has sent us an application for the post of receptionist in our hotel and given us your name as a referee. We would be most grateful if you would write a character reference for the applicant, indicating how long you have known her, and including a description of her character and the reasons why you think she might be suitable for the job. We would appreciate it if you could include at least one weakness so that we might gain a more accurate and balanced impression of the applicant.

We look forward to hearing from you.

Yours faithfully

first day at school

Strengths	Weaknesses
• really nice – very friendly	• can lose her temper unexpectedly
• great talker	• often does her own thing without considering others
• very independent-minded	• sensitive to criticism
• usually very calm and relaxed	• sometimes too talkative!

2 Read the following sample answer and comment on the following:

- the impression likely to be created by the character reference on the target reader
- the length of the note.

Dear Sir/Madam

Character reference: Anna Kaufmann

I have to say that Anna Kaufmann, who I have known since our first day at school, would be an excellent receptionist for your prestigious four-star hotel. She's a really nice, friendly person and she speaks very good English.

Firstly, though, you asked me to talk about some of her weak points. She can be a bit sensitive to criticism and sometimes she's too talkative – she was always getting into trouble at school for chatting in lessons! Also, she doesn't always consider other people or ask them for their opinion when she does things, but she'd definitely be alright working as a member of a team. I'm sure she'd change her ways for the job – I know she really wants it because she's

always wanted to go to Ireland and besides, she'll be nearer her sister, who's studying in Limerick. Apart from that, she can lose her temper unexpectedly, but I don't think she'd ever be rude to a hotel guest.

The fact is, she has a lot of positive points. She's a great talker and she's one of the most independent-minded, calm and relaxed people I've ever met. I have no hesitation in recommending her for the job. I think she'd do it very well.

Yours faithfully

Peter Schmidt

Dear Anna

I'm writing this note to let you know you that the Hotel Eire on the outskirts of Dublin has been in touch with me asking me to write a character reference for you for the job as receptionist you told me about in your last letter. Well, I've written it and I've said lots of nice things about you so I'm sure you'll get called for interview. I had to include some negative things about you, too – I won't tell you what I put! – but I think I managed to make it all sound more positive than negative.

Anyway, I just want to wish you luck with the application. Can you tell me what happens – I'm dying to know.

Bye for now

Peter

3   Decide which of the following statements about the sample answer are true (T) and which are false (F). Give reasons and/or find examples to justify your answer.

   a The writer is right to mention all of his friend's weaknesses in the character reference.

   b More emphasis should be given to the friend's positive qualities in the character reference.

   c The register is appropriate in both the character reference and the note.

   d Some of the contents of the character reference and the note are irrelevant.

   e The writer has not used his own words as much as he could.

4   **a** Negative qualities can appear less serious when mentioned together with a relevant, more positive attribute.

     eg … *and his spontaneity is a major strength. It can cause him to express his emotions at inappropriate times, but this is a small price to pay.*

   b Match each of the weaknesses in the input material to a relevant strength.

     Example: *can lose her temper unexpectedly/usually very calm and relaxed*

… and his spontaneity is a major strength. It can cause him to express his emotions at inappropriate times, but this is a small price to pay.

5   Write your own answer to the question. Aim to write a more positive character reference and a briefer note than in the sample answer.

Don't forget!

- You do not need to mention all your friend's weaknesses.
- Write in an appropriate register for each part of the task.
- Do not copy whole phrases from the input material.

Before you write

Read the following pages in the Coursebook.
Character references: pages 56 and 57 in Unit 4 and page 204 in Ready for Writing.
Notes: pages 68 and 69 in Unit 5.

Reading

Multiple matching

1 Read paragraphs **A** and **B**. In these paragraphs, the writer's tone shows that she is probably

   a sceptical regarding the use of dogs in the classroom.

   b impressed with Henry's effect on the children.

   c unconvinced that Henry is making any difference.

2 For questions **1–18**, answer by choosing from the sections of the article (**A–G**). Some of the choices may be required more than once.

In which section are the following mentioned?

increasing confidence in an aspect of academic ability	**1** ____
the criteria regarding the selection of an appropriate dog	**2** ____
the role of teachers in helping students achieve success	**3** ____
the claim that a dog has reduced the amount of absenteeism	**4** ____
a motivating reason for students to keep up with their school work	**5** ____ **6** ____
evidence to back up the theory that dogs can improve physical well-being	**7** ____
the celebrity status that a dog has recently acquired	**8** ____
people eventually being persuaded that a dog at school is beneficial	**9** ____ **10** ____
a misunderstanding concerning the treatment of a dog	**11** ____
a dog's popularity not attracting negative feelings	**12** ____
the inability to explain how a dog can have a relaxing effect	**13** ____
the writer's expectation of an unfavourable reaction	**14** ____
a decision which was taken to avoid provoking people	**15** ____
the accusation that schools have dogs just to attract media attention	**16** ____
a welcome positive effect on a group of people that Wendy Brown had not anticipated	**17** ____
the fundamental reason why dogs can have a positive impact on people's happiness	**18** ____

Paws for thought

*Buying a dog for a school isn't a barking mad idea, says Mary Braid.
Man's best friend is also a useful classroom assistant.*

A Henry is the undisputed star of Dronfield school near Sheffield. Whatever the achievements of other members of the comprehensive school, it is Henry with his soulful eyes and glossy hair, who has hogged the limelight, appearing on television in Britain and abroad. Yet despite all the public adulation, Henry stirs up no envy or resentment among the 2,000 students at Dronfield High – in fact, they all adore him. The pupils say the Cavalier King Charles spaniel is simply a pupil's best friend. Their teachers make even bigger assertions for Henry. They say the dog, who first bounded into Dronfield six months ago, is a super dog, who has improved pupil behaviour, attendance records and academic achievement.

B "It's hard not to drift off in class sometimes," explains Andrew Wainwright, 15, who like everyone else, is mushy about Henry. "So I take time out of class three or four times a week to catch up on work and Henry is always in the room I go to. He helps me focus and get on with it." Andrew says Henry is a calming influence. He can't put his finger on it, but says there's something magical about being able to throw Henry a soft toy or have Henry pad up and lick his hand while he is studying. "If we fall behind, Miss Brown won't let us look after him or feed him treats, and everyone wants to walk Henry."

C Wendy Brown is Andrew's teacher. It was Brown and Julie Smart, the school counsellor, who first floated the notion of buying a school dog. "Julie and I grew up with dogs and we were talking one day about how looking after dogs can affect children's conduct," says Brown. She says that initially other staff members thought the suggestion was ludicrous. "But we did some research and discovered that the presence of pets has been shown to be therapeutic. It's been found that animals improve recovery after surgery or illness and have a calming influence on people in lots of settings. Some of my kids can be a handful and some of the children Julie counsels have terrific problems. We thought a dog might help and other staff have now come round to that."

D The two teachers could have plucked a dog from a rescue centre but felt that those dogs were more likely to have difficulties. What they and what troubled children needed was a stable, intelligent, people-loving animal. Step forward puppy Henry, purchased from a local breeder. Julie looks after him after school hours – information that has calmed the animal lovers who complained to the school about Henry's treatment. "They seemed to think we locked him in a school cupboard overnight," says Brown. "In fact, Henry's lot is a luxurious one. The school budget was too tight to buy a dog and you can imagine that putting one before books might have stirred some people up a bit. We wanted the least controversy possible so we settled on approaching local churches. They donated the funds to buy him and his favourite food."

E Today Henry is on Dronfield's front line when it comes to helping children struggling with everything from attention deficit disorder to a sudden death in the family. In the next few weeks, the dog will launch his own confidential counselling website, *Ask Henry*. Pupils will be encouraged to log in with problems and Julie will answer on Henry's behalf. Wouldn't teenagers run horrified from such a scheme? Apparently not when Henry is involved! "Henry has been a massive success," insists Brown, explaining that even the most doubting staff have finally been won round. Perhaps that is because Henry, who lies on the floor during staff meetings, has also had a calming influence on teachers. "Not part of the plan," says Brown, "but a very welcome benefit."

F Could the school dog become a craze? Brown has already been contacted by eight schools keen to get their own dog. Other schools such as the Mulberry Bush, a primary school for 36 children with emotional and behavioural problems, have stepped forward to point out they already have one. Rosie Johnston, a Mulberry staff member, first brought her golden retriever, Muskoka, into school when he was just nine weeks old. That was three years ago. Aside from being a calming influence, Muskoka even plays his part in literacy lessons. Children at the school can be too shy to read to adults so they read to Muskoka. "Their anxiety about making mistakes is reduced when they read to him," says Johnston. "If they can maintain reasonable grades, they also get to groom and feed him. That's a big incentive."

G Psychologist Dr Deborah Wells from Queen's University Belfast specializes in animal–human interaction and is not surprised about the claims made for Henry or Muskoka. She believes the underlying key to the Henry effect is that dogs offer unconditional love and that cheers up adults and children and helps with self-esteem. But traditionalist Chris Woodhead, the former chief inspector of schools, says that he has encountered his fair share of pets, but never a dog. "I can see how children with behavioural difficulties might be helped, but I'm sceptical about the use of dogs in the mainstream," says Woodhead. "I don't see why a teacher cannot create a positive learning environment through the subject they teach and their personality. Dogs strike me as a bit of a publicity stunt." But Henry remains as popular as ever. He's just become the first animal to be made an honorary member of the public services union Unison – in recognition of his services as a canine classroom assistant.

Vocabulary

Wordlist on page 212 of the Coursebook.

A Sleep

Complete each of the gaps with one of the words from the box.

| off |
| into |
| on |
| over |
| from |
| through |
| to |
| up |

1 The neighbours had a party last night and we didn't **get** _____ **sleep** till about 3.

2 I **stayed** _____ to watch the boxing last night – it started just after midnight.

3 Our daughter still doesn't **sleep** _____ **the night** – she always wakes up at least once.

4 She went to bed exhausted and immediately **fell** _____ **a deep sleep**.

5 The review of his performance was far from complimentary, but he wasn't going to **lose any sleep** _____ **it**.

6 I'm going to **sleep** _____ **it** tonight and I'll let you know my decision tomorrow.

7 I couldn't tell you what happened – I **nodded** _____ just before the end of the film.

8 A surprisingly high percentage of the population **suffers** _____ **insomnia**.

B Abilities

Match each sentence beginning **1–6** with an appropriate ending **a–f**.

1 This highly talented artist has **an eye**

2 Realizing he did not have **a good ear**

3 The young reporter clearly had **a nose**

4 He admits that he doesn't have **a head**

5 Dave did it himself; he is **a dab hand**

6 Being bilingual he has **a natural flair**

a **for figures**, and he leaves all the accounting work to his wife, Pam.

b **for music**, he gave up trying to learn the piano and took up acting instead.

c **for languages**, and has taught himself Russian, Greek and Polish.

d **for detail** and many of his works are mistaken for photographs.

e **for a good story** and he wrote several exclusives for the popular tabloid.

f **at DIY** and wouldn't dream of getting a builder in to do anything.

Self help

Study the expressions in bold in B for one minute. Then cover the sentence endings a–f and look only at the beginnings 1–6. How many expressions can you remember?

C Adjectives in film reviews

Match each of the adjectives to an appropriate description.

| moving | gripping | stunning | innovative |
| clichéd | over-hyped | excruciating | unconvincing |

1 Both the plot and the characters were difficult to believe. _____

2 It contains some very new and original animation techniques. _____

3 We've seen this type of thing so many times before. _____

4 It had me on the edge of my seat. _____

5 It didn't live up to the expectations created by all the publicity. _____

6 Take a big box of tissues to this one – you'll need them. _____

7 Painful to watch; the most boring film of the year. _____

8 She gave an amazing performance – her most impressive yet. _____

Language focus

 Grammar reference on page 220 of the Coursebook.

1 In **1–5** below, decide which sentence, **a** or **b**, follows on more naturally from the first sentence.

1 Captain John Simms, the controversial chairman of league leaders Greendale United, is in the news again.

  a The 59-year-old former ex-Army officer **has announced** his intention to cut players' wages by 10% if they fail to win their semi-final cup match against neighbours Bromwich City on Saturday.

  b The intention to cut players' wages by 10% if they fail to win their semi-final cup match against neighbours Bromwich City on Saturday **has been announced** by the 59-year-old ex-Army officer.

2 After Paris, this magnificent collection of paintings moves to the Reina Sofia Museum in Madrid, where it will remain until January.

  a A number of leading financial organizations, including two major Spanish banks and the French insurance giant ULP, which devotes 1% of its profits to the arts, **have sponsored** the exhibition.

  b The exhibition **has been sponsored** by a number of leading financial organizations, including two major Spanish banks and the French insurance giant ULP, which devotes 1% of its profits to the arts.

3 Annette Sawyer is the brainiest student in town!

  a The people marking her GCSE examination papers **have awarded** the sixteen-year-old from Brayton High School top marks in all eleven of her exams, a record for any pupil from Tipton, past or present.

  b The sixteen-year-old from Brayton High School **has been awarded** top marks in all eleven of her GCSE exams, a record for any pupil from Tipton, past or present.

4 The driver of a delivery van is recovering in hospital from head injuries sustained in a curious incident which occurred in the centre of Worthing yesterday.

  a Paul Roberts of Kingston Lane, Shoreham, was on his way home when he **crashed into** a lorry parked outside the main post office in Harper Street.

  b A lorry parked outside the main post office in Harper Street **was crashed into** by Paul Roberts of Kingston Lane, Shoreham, as he was on his way home.

5 Everything is done to ensure maximum comfort and relaxation for our guests during their stay at the Wilton Hotel.

  a The cleaners **do not** come in to **clean** your room until 11am each day, so as not to disturb you.

  b Rooms **are not cleaned** until 11am each day in order to avoid possible disturbance.

Everything is done to ensure maximum comfort and relaxation for our guests during their stay at the Wilton Hotel.

2 Complete the second sentence so that it has a similar meaning to the first sentence. There is an example at the beginning **(0)**.

0 Everyone knows she is a close friend of the Prime Minister.

She *is known to be a close friend of the Prime Minister.*

1 It is understood that the company is planning a takeover bid for its rival.

The company _____ .

2 Police say the offences took place on Monday.

The offences _____ .

3 It is believed that the injured motorcyclist was travelling at over 100 mph.

The injured _____ .

4 Experts thought that infected chickens were responsible for the outbreak of flu.

Infected chickens _____ .

5 They alleged she had lied in order to protect her boyfriend.

She _____ .

6 Someone stole my camera last weekend.

I had _____ .

7 Your eyes need testing.

You need _____ .

8 My foot became stuck in the hole.

I _____ .

English in Use

CAE Part 2

Open cloze

For questions **1–15**, complete the following article by writing **one** word in each space. The exercise begins with an example **(0)**.

Snoring

Sleep deprivation can make us very angry, which is **(0)** *why* snoring – the human equivalent of a car alarm **(1)** _____ set off at night – can be so irritating. Most people snore occasionally, but in middle age about 40 per cent of men and 20 per cent of women **(2)** _____ so regularly. Snoring can ruin relationships and be intensely embarrassing. Snorers **(3)** _____ go into hospital, for example, may worry that they'll keep the whole ward awake. But snoring doesn't **(4)** _____ afflict the unafflicted; snorers may also disturb **(5)** _____ and feel sleepy during the day.

Snoring can sometimes be a symptom of a more serious condition. Up **(6)** _____ six per cent of men and two per cent of women suffer from sleep apnoea, a syndrome in which breathing **(7)** _____ significantly disrupted during sleep. Some people may start off **(8)** _____ uncomplicated snorers, but develop sleep apnoea as they get older. The word apnoea is derived **(9)** _____ the Greek and means "no breathing". People **(10)** _____ sleep apnoea have airways that become obstructed during sleep. Typically, they snore loudly, stop breathing, struggle **(11)** _____ air, partly wake up (although often unaware of it), gulp a bit, and then recommence snoring. The cycle may **(12)** _____ repeated over 100 times an hour.

(13) _____ surprisingly, people with sleep apnoea feel unrefreshed in the morning. They may have problems concentrating during the day, feel depressed and fall asleep **(14)** _____ socially unacceptable times. At worst, they can fall asleep **(15)** _____ driving or operating dangerous machinery.

CAE Part 4 **Word formation**

For questions **1–10** use the words in the box to form **one** word that fits in the same numbered space in the text. The exercise begins with an example **(0)**.

Genetic genius

According to a recent study the best **(0)** _musicians_ are born, not made. **(1)** _____ at St Thomas's Hospital in London claim that genes are responsible for up to 80 per cent of our ability to recognize pitch, the key to musical **(2)** _____ . In a 'distorted tunes test' over 500 twins were played a **(3)** _____ of popular songs, each **(4)** _____ a number of errors. A **(5)** _____ of the **(6)** _____ of identical twins with those of non-identical twins revealed that the former were **(7)** _____ better at spotting the mistakes. The results of the study suggest that for some children, music lessons may only go so far in improving musical abilities such as pitch **(8)** _____ . However, parents hoping to save money on lessons cannot use the test as an early indicator of musical potential: it is **(9)** _____ for children under 12, who do not have sufficient **(10)** _____ of the tunes played.

0	MUSIC
1	RESEARCH
2	GREAT
3	VARY
4	CONTAIN
5	COMPARE
6	RESPOND
7	NOTICE
8	RECOGNIZE
9	RELY
10	KNOW

Writing

CAE Part 2 **Article**

1 Read the following Writing Part 2 task and the two versions of the same article below. Which of the versions is more likely to be published? Give reasons for your answer.

You see the announcement below in _Live and Learn_, an international magazine.

The best days of your life?

We invite you, our readers, to submit an article on the secondary school you used to attend or are attending now.

We'd like you to:
- tell us about the positive and negative aspects of your secondary school
- give your overall opinion of the education you received or are receiving
- say how typical the school was or is of other schools in your country.

We will publish the most interesting article from each country.

Write your **article** in approximately 250 words.

Version A

My school

In my secondary school the teachers were very strict and they did not allow us to talk at all during the lessons. They used boring teaching methods like dictation, and they were not very friendly towards the pupils.

To show how superior they were, the teachers always addressed us by our surname and many wore the traditional cap and gown in class. They thought that they had all the knowledge and we would learn just by listening to them. They were all men; there were no women teachers in our school. Other schools in the country had a more progressive type of education, the students did more in lessons and there were mixed ability classes. My school and a few others like it still had passive learning and iron discipline.

However, students got good marks, except the ones who did not behave well. There were a lot of students who were good at sport and the sports facilities were very good. We had a swimming pool and squash courts, and a language laboratory and some video recorders. Every year some of the rich students went to Interlaken in Switzerland.

But I don't think my school prepared me very well for the world of work. I also think the education wasn't general enough and it didn't teach me to think for myself.

49

Version B

> ## Distance learning: formal address in formal dress
>
> "Cease this idle chatter, boys; there will be no talking. I shall dictate and you will write." This was an all too common instruction at the secondary school I had the misfortune to attend, and helps to illustrate the teaching methods used and the distance that teachers liked to keep from their pupils.
>
> They always addressed us by our surname and, as if to demonstrate their superiority further, many would regularly wear the traditional cap and gown in class. The teacher was the source of all knowledge, and his students — this was an all-male institution — merely empty vessels to be filled. Whilst the trend up and down the country was towards a more progressive type of education, with greater student involvement and mixed ability classes, my own school and a few others like it, seemed trapped in a time bubble of passive learning and iron discipline.
>
> Having said all that, I cannot deny that academic achievement was high, provided, of course, you didn't rebel against the system. And the school's many talented young sportsmen were able to make use of its extensive sports facilities. Indeed, unlike most other schools at the time, ours boasted a swimming pool and squash courts, as well as a language laboratory and a number of video recorders. There was even an annual trip to Interlaken in Switzerland — for those whose parents could afford it.
>
> But how many of us can say we were adequately prepared for the world of work which awaited us? How many of us can claim we ended our schooldays as fully rounded individuals capable of thinking for ourselves? I'm not sure I can.

2 Identify the part or parts of **Version B** in which each of the following are mentioned:

   a the positive aspects of the school
   b the negative aspects of the school
   c his overall opinion of the education he received
   d how typical the school was of others in his country

3   Write your own answer to the question. Before you do, complete the exercises in
A and B below.

A Planning

1   When planning your answer you might consider some of the following
main categories:

Facilities	Teachers	Academic achievement	Extra-curricular activities
Discipline	Teaching and learning methods		Range of subjects

In 1–7, match each of the main categories to the related ideas. The first one has been
done for you.

Main categories	Related ideas
1 _Teachers_ :	knowledge, skills, ability to motivate, empathy
2 _____ :	theoretical or practical, variety, student involvement, interest
3 _____ :	types of punishment and their effectiveness
4 _____ :	wide or limited, broad education or specialization
5 _____ :	exam results, school's 'success'
6 _____ :	buildings, equipment eg computers, laboratories etc
7 _____ :	clubs, societies, sporting activities, excursions, holidays

2   Which of these categories are mentioned in **Version B**?

B Beginnings and endings

1   What techniques are used to begin and end **Version B**?

2   Match each of the article beginnings 1–5 with a technique in the box.

An unusual statement	A fact or statistic	A question
A story	A comparison	

1
According to recent figures, there is a computer for every six
secondary school pupils in this country. Clearly, those who
compiled these figures did not visit my school, where there are
over a thousand pupils and no more than a dozen computers.

2
Have you ever wondered how different your life might have
been if you'd gone to a different school? I know I have,
and it makes me realize just how fortunate I was to attend
St Cuthbert's comprehensive in Pencaster.

3
A terrified young boy walks into the headmaster's office and receives six
strokes of the cane – as punishment for talking in class. Ten years later the
same boy, a young man now, walks into the courtroom and receives a
15-year prison sentence – as punishment for a vicious assault. I wonder how
many more violent criminals were the product of brutal regimes at school.

4
There's nothing like a gentle ear massage and a short session
of air writing with your nose to refresh the mind before a
session on geometry. 'Brain breaks' such as these were an
integral part of my schooling and I cannot speak highly
enough of them.

5
You wouldn't ask an ex-convict if he enjoyed his
spell in jail. And you probably wouldn't ask a
recently discharged patient whether she had a
good time in hospital. So please don't ask me if
I enjoyed my 7 years at Hove County Grammar
School for Boys!

Don't forget!

- Plan your answer using the ideas in 3 A above.
- Engage the reader's interest in the first paragraph using one of the techniques in 3 B above.
- End the article in an interesting or thought-provoking way.
- Use a range of vocabulary and structures.
- Give your article a title which reflects the content of the article.

Now you are ready to write your article.

Reading

CAE Part 2

Gapped text

1 For questions **1–6**, choose which of the paragraphs **A–G** on page 53 fit into the gaps in the following magazine article. There is one extra paragraph which does not fit in any of the gaps.

The boy who broke every rule in the book

Was Nicholas Culpeper a medical rebel who challenged the establishment, or simply a quack? Scarlett Thomas asks.

Anyone who has ever rubbed dock leaf on a nettle sting, used peppermint tea to ease indigestion or taken chamomile for a good night's sleep has been using herbal medicine. However suspicious some of us may be of a complete system of 'alternative' healing, we all know that, for example, vinegar is good on wasp stings, and honey helps a sore throat.

1	

These are questions which have persisted for centuries. Who has the right to medical knowledge? And how could you make sure you were in safe hands? It is to the 16th century, with its complex medical system of grandmothers, quacks, mid-wives, apothecaries and a few physicians, that Benjamin Woolley first takes us in his immensely readable book *The Herbalist*. We learn of Henry VIII's answer to the problem of regulation: the creation of the *College of Physicians*, the members of which were given licensing and fining powers – but not the power to dispense medicines, which was instead held by the apothecaries.

2	

Although they were supposed to practice only in accordance with the *Pharmacopoeia Londinensis*, a huge book of instructions and recipes created by the *College of Physicians*, most apothecaries did not actually read Latin. This inability meant that they could not in fact read the book.

3	

Even without Latin, most apothecaries had some idea of what their medicines did. And despite not understanding the attack on their characters in the *Pharmacopoeia*, the apothecaries also knew that the College had it in for them. In 1634, Nicholas Culpeper, aged 18, arrived in London with £50 in his pocket, looking for an apprenticeship. He soon became an apprentice to an apothecary, becoming familiar with long lists of 'simple' ingredients set out in the *Pharmacopoeia*, including bizarre items like excrement of wolf, human blood, crayfish eyes, sweat, ass milk and 'intestines of the earth', in other words, earthworms.

4	

So eventually abandoning his apprenticeship and despite all the rules created by the *College of Physicians*, Culpepper set up on his own as an 'independent', trading out of a shop in London's Threadneedle Street. His aim was to provide medical help for anyone who needed it, however poor, and to treat people with simply prepared, locally sourced medicines, not the exotic concoctions favoured by the *College*. This career was interrupted by a stint as a soldier in the Civil War. It was shortly after it ended that there was a widespread call for all legal matters to be conducted in English, so justice could be heard and understood by all.

5	

When it appeared, it was twice as long as the original, bulging with additions and corrections. It also explained what the recipes were for. "In translating the book," Woolley notes, "Nicholas broke every rule in it." This was seen not just as a medical act, but a deeply political one. The *College of Physicians* was outraged.

6	

Was Culpeper a quack? No more so than the medical establishment of the time, argues Woolley. It was the *College's Pharmacopoeia* after all that recommended the use of the treatments based on ground gall stones of Persian goats that surely led to King Charles II's demise. Yet Culpeper's legacy – the idea that medicine is not something that should be controlled and administered by the elite but something belonging to everybody – is as important and, perhaps, as revolutionary, now as it was in the 17th century.

* a quack = a negative term to describe someone who pretends to possess medical knowledge and acts as a doctor

A Perhaps this was fortunate, as it warned of 'a dangerous plague which our book will counteract, namely the very noxious fraud or deceit of those people who are allowed to sell the most filthy concoctions, and even mud, under the name and title of medicaments for the sake of profit'.

B As odd as these may seem, many recipes would also call for the drug opium, which at the time, cost less than garden rhubarb. Culpeper did not have a good experience at this time, being assigned a new master on several occasions. Then again, this was probably not a good time for anyone to be in his position, when rules meant you could be summoned to a company 'court' for having 'stubbornness and long hair'.

C *The English Physician*, Culpeper's later book, better known as *Culpeper's Complete Herbal*, did little to pacify them. It outlined not only the uses and features of healing plants but also Culper's holistic view of medicine. Despite upsetting the establishment, it became one of the most popular and enduring books in British history.

D When things get more serious, of course, most people rush to the doctor. But what if the doctor gets it wrong? Or imagine a situation when, for whatever reasons, you wanted to find out how to use other plants to heal yourself or your own family.

E Mutual distrust and rivalry between these groups seem to have defined the medical system of the next 100 years. It wasn't until the great plague that things were shaken up. London was left almost empty of doctors, with only apothecaries still providing medical care.

F It reveals a profound insight into the trade practices and monopolies of the time, and how the establishment view of who should be allowed to trade and under what conditions affects everything. This was especially true concerning the health of people denied control over their medical treatment.

G Impressed by this, Culpeper's thoughts turned to a similar democratisation of medical texts. These thoughts would be made reality when he was commissioned to produce an English edition of the *Pharmacopoeia*.

2 Look at these two sentences from the text. What is the meaning of the phrasal verbs in bold?

[Culpepper became] familiar with long lists of 'simple' ingredients *set out* in the *Pharmacopoeia*.

[He] *set up* on his own as an 'independent', trading out of a shop in London's Threadneedle Street.

3 Match each of the phrasal verbs in sentences **1–7** with an appropriate definition **a–g**.

Example: 1 c

1 Let's stay at home – it looks as though the rain's **set in** for the day.

2 I put on my old clothes and **set about** clearing out the garden shed.

3 You should aim to **set aside** at least 15 minutes each day for physical exercise.

4 Strike action **set back** the building of the Olympic stadium by several weeks.

5 We **set off** at 6 in the morning and got there just before midday.

6 It is the quality of her writing which **sets** her **apart** from other children's authors.

7 No sooner had he jumped down into the garden than he was **set upon** by two enormous guard dogs.

a delay the progress of something

b start doing something

c start and seem likely to continue

d attack somebody

e reserve time for a specific purpose

f make somebody different from others

g start a journey

Vocabulary

Wordlist on page 213 of the Coursebook.

Phrasal verbs

Complete each gap with the appropriate form of one of the verbs from the box. In each section, **1–6**, the verb required for both spaces, **a** and **b**, is the same. There is an example at the beginning **(0)**.

wear	put	~~pass~~	break
come	get	bring	

0 a He _passed_ **out** at the sight of blood, and didn't regain consciousness for over a minute.
  b I took the day off work – I didn't want to _pass_ my cold **on** to everyone there.

1 a He suffered a heart attack, which may have been _____ **on** by stress.
  b She was unconscious, so I threw water over her face in an attempt to _____ her **round**.

2 a My energy levels are low, and I feel absolutely _____ **out** when I get home from work.
  b I started to feel pain as the effects of the drug began to _____ **off**.

3 a I fully intended to go to the dentist's last month, but I never _____ **round to** making an appointment.
  b I hope I _____ **over** this flu soon – I don't want to be ill when I go on holiday.

4 a The cholera epidemic _____ **out** in Peru in January 1991 and spread rapidly to neighbouring countries.
  b I'm allergic to dairy products; if I eat any, I _____ **out in** a nasty rash.

5 a I'm in agony – I tried to lift up the television on my own and I _____ my back **out**.
  b She was suffering from an upset stomach, which she _____ **down to** the fish she'd eaten the night before.

6 a Denise has just phoned from her sick bed – she's _____ **down with** a flu bug, apparently.
  b Scientists have yet to _____ **up with** the definitive cure for baldness.

Word formation

1 Complete the table with the infinitives of the verbs formed from the words in the box. The first two have been done for you.

~~sure~~	~~strong~~	courage	deaf	high	danger
deep	rich	broad	sad	force	

-en	en-
strengthen	_ensure_

2 Complete each of the gaps using the appropriate form of the word in capitals at the
end of the line. There is an example at the beginning (0).

0 In an effort to *ensure* **success** in next year's European competition, United **SURE**
have *strengthened* their **team** by buying two outstanding overseas players. **STRONG**

1 The build-up of troops in the border area has _____ **tension** **HIGH**
between the two countries.

2 Faced with a rapidly _____ economic **crisis**, the Prime Minister **DEEP**
was coming under increasing pressure to resign.

3 Despite rocketing unemployment figures, the President insisted **COURAGE**
that there were some _____ **signs** of recovery in the economy.

4 Join the World Wildlife Fund and help protect _____ **species** **DANGER**
from extinction.

5 The FBI is perhaps the best known of America's **law** _____ **FORCE**
agencies.

6 She was **deeply** _____ by the death of her cat. **SAD**

7 There is no doubt that the school's work experience programme **BROAD**
_____ **the outlook** of its pupils and greatly _____ **their lives**. **RICH**

8 His audience found the joke offensive and greeted it with
a _____ **silence**. **DEAF**

Language focus

 Grammar reference on page 221 of the Coursebook.

Reported speech

1 Cross out the two options which **cannot** be used to complete each sentence. There is
an example at the beginning (0).

0 The doctor *reassured*/~~explained~~/*promised*/~~mentioned~~ her that the drugs would have
no serious side-effects.

1 She *invited/refused/offered/asked* me to go on holiday with her.

2 David *denied/admitted/confessed/claimed* to being a little nervous before the
operation.

3 We were *accused/blamed/told off/complained* for causing the disruption.

4 My mother *persuaded/encouraged/insisted/requested* I go with her to the hospital.

5 Several people have *commented/complimented/remarked/congratulated* on Sally's
new look.

6 Zoe's beautician *advised/suggested/argued/warned* her against having cosmetic
surgery.

7 We tried to *dissuade/discourage/urge/convince* her from going through with it, as
well.

8 It has been *told/assured/announced/confirmed* that the security forces will be on
maximum alert.

9 My boss could see I was stressed out and he *advised/suggested/proposed/recommended*
me to take a few days' holiday.

10 She found a dead spider in her salad and *demanded/ordered/asked/insisted* to see
the manager.

2   Rewrite each sentence in two different ways. In each gap you should write **between two and four words**. There is an example at the beginning **(0)**.

0 "I'll help you do your homework later," she told him.

   a She said that _she would help him_ do his homework later.

   b She promised _to help him_ do his homework later.

1 "I'll cut you out of my will if you marry George," he told his daughter.

   a He said that _____ his daughter out of his will if she married George.

   b He threatened _____ his daughter out of his will if she married George.

2 "I think you should take a few days off work," he told me.

   a He said he _____ a few days off work.

   b He suggested _____ a few days off work.

3 "You must leave immediately!" she told them.

   a She said that _____ immediately.

   b She ordered _____ immediately.

4 "I've always loved you," he told her.

   a He said that _____ her.

   b He confessed to _____ her.

5 "It wasn't me who stole it," she insisted.

   a She insisted that she _____ .

   b She denied _____ .

6 There's a rumour that they paid her over $3 million for her part in the film.

   a It is rumoured that she _____ over $3 million for her part in the film.

   b She is rumoured _____ over $3 million for her part in the film.

7 "Can you take my name off the list?" he asked her.

   a He asked her if _____ his name off the list.

   b He requested that _____ be included on the list.

8 "Aliens abducted me," he told journalists.

   a He assured journalists that he _____ by aliens.

   b He claimed to _____ by aliens.

'It wasn't me who stole it,' she insisted.

English in Use

Error correction

In **most** lines of the following text there is **one** unnecessary word. It is **either** grammatically incorrect **or** does not fit in with the sense of the text. If a line is correct, put a tick (✔) in the space at the end of the line. If a line has an unnecessary word, write the word in the space. The exercise begins with two examples **(0)** and **(00)**.

Don't forget!

Read the text through first. Your understanding of the overall context may affect some of your choices.

Hospital plasters wrong leg

0	A two-year-old girl has taken to hospital with a broken right leg had	*has*
00	her left leg put in plaster. Alexandra Dignum was taken to Medway	✓
1	Maritime Hospital after her mother, Louise, noticed her own right	_____
2	leg was swollen. Alexandra's father said that the mistake which was	_____
3	discovered only when the family returned at home. "Louise and I	_____
4	have looked at one another in disbelief when we realized they had	_____
5	plastered the wrong leg. We would like complain officially, but they	_____
6	are so disorganized they would probably file the complaint in the	_____
7	wrong tray." He added that if the two plaster casts were so heavy	_____
8	he could barely lift his daughter. Ms Dignum said that she regretted	_____
9	not noticing the mistake at once, but "you have to have had some	_____
10	faith that the professionals know what they are doing". A spokesman	_____
11	for the hospital explained that the note was given to Alexandra's	_____
12	mother to take to the plaster room was not only legible. He said:	_____
13	"This led to the plaster technician questioning the mother as to which	_____
14	leg was most affected. The mother indicated it was the left leg and	_____
15	this was also plastered. She was later brought back and the correct	_____
16	plaster was being applied. We deeply regret the error and will be	_____
	reviewing our procedures."	

CAE Part 6

Gapped text

For questions **1–6**, read the following text and then choose from the list (**A–I**) the best phrase given below it to fill each of the spaces. Each correct phrase may be used only once. Some of the suggested answers do not fit at all.

Working out

Exercise isn't just about looking good and losing weight; it's probably the best thing we can do **(1)** _____ and make sure we reach our eighties in fine form. Our bodies were built to move. Without exercise they fall apart.

A well-rounded workout will promote cardiovascular fitness, muscular strength and endurance, flexibility, balance and agility. Many regular gym users will happily use the bike, treadmill or cross trainer which are great for cardio but they'll largely ignore the top half of their bodies – arms, neck and top of the back. There are plenty of machines **(2)** _____ , but free weights will give the best results because you're using more of your body than you do on a machine that concentrates on just one muscle group. However, do get a professional **(3)** _____ because it's important to learn the right lifting techniques to avoid injury.

If you have back problems, using a Swiss ball when you're exercising will help **(4)** _____ . You can place it between you and a wall, for example, and roll down it until you're in a squatting position. It's also fun **(5)** _____ while you're lifting weights because not only are your arms being used but your abdomen will be working hard to keep you from falling off.

If you dislike gym sessions, there are usually plenty of classes that come free with your membership fee. *T'ai chi*, for example, is a perfect way to improve your shape because it teaches poise. Good deportment creates the illusion of a taller and slimmer frame. *Body pump* is a popular newcomer and now reckoned **(6)** _____ . It's a complex workout performed to music using barbells with adjustable weights and suitable for all levels of fitness.

A to help you do this
B to show you how to use them
C to be the quickest way to get in shape
D to try to balance on one
E to play with them

F to prolong our lives
G to protect it
H to work these parts
I to be much better for you

Writing

CAE Part 2

Review

1 Read the following Writing Part 2 task.

The magazine published by your English club has asked its readers to send in a review of a film or book which includes a sporting theme. Write a review for the magazine commenting on the importance of the sporting theme in the film or book and saying how well you think it is handled. You should also say why you think others might or might not enjoy seeing the film or reading the book.

2 Read the following answer, ignoring the gaps for the moment. Does the review address all parts of the task?

10 years in the life of Muhammad Ali

'I AM THE GREATEST!' exclaims Will Smith in the **(1)** _____ role of this compelling film about the former world heavyweight boxing champion. But these words apply equally well to Smith's own extremely powerful acting **(2)** _____ as the man who was named sportsperson of the century in several countries including his own. Smith looks, moves and talks like the legendary boxer, and his well-deserved Oscar **(3)** _____ for Best Actor is reason enough to see the film.

Boxing is clearly central to the film, which is **(4)** _____ in the period from Ali's title-winning defeat of Sonny Liston in 1964 to his regaining of the crown from George Foreman a decade later. To the untrained eye, the boxing **(5)** _____ are entirely convincing, and succeed in conveying both the passion and the horror of the sport. The film builds up to a dramatic **(6)** _____ with the 1974 fight in Zaire,

and the combination of Michael Mann's expert direction and the moving musical **(7)** _____ makes this one of the most memorable moments of the film.

But don't be put off if you're not a boxing fan – the film is as much about the social context in which the **(8)** _____ takes place as about heavyweight fights. It provides a fascinating **(9)** _____ into nineteen sixties America and Ali's response to contemporary attitudes. It explores his relationship with the black Muslims and also shows how he risked his career and his freedom by refusing induction into the army at the time of the Vietnam War.

There's something for everyone in the film: sport, history, drama, romance and even humour. Many of the boxer's witty **(10)** _____ , particularly those delivered to journalists, will have you laughing out loud and developing an affection for one of the world's truly great sporting heroes.

3   Complete each of the gaps with one of the words from the box.

scenes	lines	insight	action
performance	set	title	nomination
climax	score		

4   Underline those adjectives used by the writer to express an opinion on the film or the acting. Underline any accompanying adverbs or nouns.

Example: compelling film

5   What other expressions are used by the writer to encourage readers to see the film?

6   Either: **a** write your own answer to the task in exercise 1
or: **b** answer the following question:

The magazine published by your English club has asked its readers to send in a review of a film or book whose content is largely biographical. Write a review for the magazine commenting on what you learnt from the film or book and saying why you think others might or might not enjoy it.

Write your **review** in approximately 250 words.

Don't forget!

- **Do not** write a long summary of the film or book.
- **Do** express your opinion throughout the review.

Before you write

In the Coursebook read page 76 in Unit 6 and page 203 in Ready for Writing.

Reading

Multiple choice

1 Read the following magazine article about the Internet and people's honesty. Answer questions **1–6** by choosing a letter **A, B, C** or **D**. Give only one answer to each question.

The web promotes honesty.

The truth is out there on the net

Far from encouraging mass deceit, the web promotes honesty because we fear getting caught, writes Clive Thompson.

Everyone tells a little white lie now and then but Cornell University professor, Jeffrey Hancock, recently claimed to have established the truth of a curious proposition: we fib less frequently when we're online than when talking in person. He asked thirty undergraduates to record all their communications, and all their lies for a week. When he tallied the results, he found the students had mishandled the truth in about one-quarter of all face-to-face conversations, and in a whopping 37 per cent of phone calls. But when they went into cyberspace, only 1 in 5 instant-messaging chats contained a lie, and barely 14 per cent of email messages were dishonest. Obviously, you can't make generalisations about society solely on the basis of college students' behaviour, and there's also something odd about asking people to be honest about how often they lie. But still, Professor Hancock's results were intriguing, not least because they upend some of our primary expectations about life on the net.

Wasn't cyberspace supposed to be the scary zone where you couldn't trust anyone? Back when the Internet first went mainstream, those pundits in the government, media and academia worried that the digital age would open the floodgates of deception. Since anyone could hide behind an anonymous hotmail address or chat-room nickname, net users, we were warned, would be free to lie with impunity. Parents panicked and frantically supervised their children's use of cyberspace, under the assumption that anyone lurking out there in the unknown was a threat until proved otherwise. And to a certain extent, you can see their reasoning: if we go along with the basic introduction to any psychology course, we're more likely to lie to people when there's distance between us. Eventually, though, all those suspicions turned out to be unfounded.

What is it, then, about online life that makes us more truthful? It's simple: we're worried about being exposed. In 'real' life, after all, it's pretty easy to get away with deception. If you lie to someone at a party, you can always claim you said no such thing. On the Internet, your words often come back to haunt you. The digital age is tough on liars, as an endless parade of executives are finding out. This isn't a problem for only corporate barons. We read the headlines; we know in cyberspace our words never die, because machines don't forget. "It's a cut-and-paste culture," as Professor Hancock put it, though he said that on the phone, so who knows if he really meant it? And consider that many email programs automatically 'quote' your words when someone replies to your message. Every time I finish an email message, I pause for a few seconds to reread it just to ensure I haven't said something I'll later regret.

Maybe this helps explain why television programmes like *CSI: Crime Scene Investigation* have become so popular. They're all about revealing the sneaky things that people do. We watch with fascination and unease as scientists inspect the tiniest of clues – a stray hair on a car seat, a latent fingerprint on a CD-ROM. After you've seen high-tech cops rake over evidence from a crime scene with ultraviolet light and luminal and genetic sequencers enough times, you get the message: Watch out – we've got files on you. Forensic science has become the central drama of pop culture, and our fascination with it may well add to our anxieties about technology. So no wonder we're so careful to restrict our lying to low-technology environments. We have begun to be keenly suspicious of places that might be bugged, conducting all of our subterfuge in loud restaurants and lonely parks.

Still, it's not only the fear of electronic exposure that drives us to tell the truth. There's something about the Internet that encourages us to 'tell all', often in rather outrageous ways. Psychologists have noticed for years that going online seems to have a catalytic effect on people's personalities. The most quiet and reserved people may become deranged loudmouths when they sit behind the keyboard. Others stay up until dawn and conduct angry debates on discussion boards with total strangers. You can usually spot the newcomers in any discussion group because they're the ones WRITING IN CAPITALS – they're overwhelmed by the Internet's heady combination of geographic distance and pseudo-invisibility.

Our impulse to confess via cyberspace inverts much of what we think about honesty. It used to be if you wanted to really trust someone, you arranged a face-to-face meeting. Our culture still obsesses over physical contact, the shaking of hands, the lubricating chitchat. Executives and politicians spend hours flying across the country merely for a five-minute meeting, on the assumption that even a few seconds of face time can cut through the prevarications of letters and legal contracts. But perhaps this growing tendency towards online communication is gratifying news. We could find ourselves living in an increasingly honest world. It will at least, inevitably, be one in which there are increasingly severe penalties for deception. With its unforgiving machine memory, the Internet might turn out to be the unlikely conscience of the world.

1 The writer states that Professor Hancock's research

   A has come up with some surprising revelations about internet use.
   B would be more valid if the participants had not known the purpose.
   C only demonstrates what was already common knowledge.
   D should have been aimed at a more reliable category of participants.

2 What does the writer state about the early days of internet use?

   A There was no discernible change in the general level of honest behaviour.
   B Parental anxiety about dishonest internet users was proven true to a degree.
   C Children were frequently not permitted any kind of access to the Internet.
   D There was widespread over-reaction to the perceived dangers of the Internet.

3 What point is illustrated by the references to email records?

   A The corporate world has been forced to reassess its systems of communication.
   B People have developed a less trusting attitude towards others they deal with.
   C People are becoming more cautious with regard to the content of email.
   D Email and similar documentation has sometimes been used to manipulate the truth.

4 According to the writer, television programmes on forensic science have

   A led to people becoming more frightened of being exposed.
   B encouraged people to adopt more sophisticated methods of deception.
   C overtaken other types of television drama in terms of popularity.
   D given people a false impression of what science can currently achieve.

5 In the fifth paragraph, what are we told about the effect of internet chatrooms on people?

   A They have had a beneficial influence on some naturally shy people.
   B They have allowed certain people to express themselves more concisely.
   C They have led to a transformation in some people's usual behaviour.
   D They have improved relations between people from different cultures.

6 What does the writer state about the future impact of online communication?

   A People will ensure that emails are strictly accurate and honest.
   B Instances of dishonesty will have more serious consequences.
   C People will feel the need for legal advice when preparing documents.
   D It will remove the need for face-to-face contact.

2   Underline the following words and expressions **1–3** in the first paragraph of the text, then match each one to it's definition **a–c**.

    1 tell a white lie   **a** an informal word meaning *to lie*

    2 fib   **b** a euphemism for *to lie*

    3 mishandle the truth   **c** to lie so as not to hurt someone's feelings

3   In **1–5** decide whether the words in bold refer to being honest (H) or dishonest (D). There is an example at the beginning **(0)**.

    0 The Minister for Education said that the newspaper's false accusations were part of a **dirty tricks campaign** designed to harm her reputation. *D*

    1 It was a remarkably **candid confession** for a politician not normally known for his readiness to own up to his mistakes.

    2 The Prime Minister accused his deputy of employing **underhand tactics** to gain control of the party by secretly encouraging other members to vote against him.

    3 Just give me a **straight answer** to a straight question: do you intend to take the exam or not?

    4 We want the advertisement to convey the message that we are a **reputable firm** of estate agents that people can trust.

    5 Hobson's **devious plan** to blackmail blameless businessmen earned him the respect of the criminal underworld.

4   Which of the adjectives in bold in **1–5** of exercise 3 above means the following:

    a dishonest and secretive

    b dishonest and clever

    c honest and reliable

    d honest and open, especially about something difficult or painful

    e honest and direct

Self help
Add the collocations in bold from exercise 3 to your vocabulary notebook.

Vocabulary

Wordlist on page 213 of the Coursebook.

Verbs formed with *up*, *down*, *over* and *under*

1   In **1–5** below, one of the four verbs is not a real word. Cross out the verb which does not exist.

    1 uproot   upgrade   uphear   update

    2 overthrow   overgo   overrule   overhear

    3 undercut   undertake   underroot   undergo

    4 upset   uphold   upstage   uprule

    5 downhold   downsize   downplay   download

2   Complete each of the gaps with one of the verbs from exercise 1. There may be more than one possible answer.

    Example: Rebels tried to <u>*overthrow*</u> the government.

    1 A higher court can _____ a judge's decision.

    2 A patient may have to _____ an operation.

    3 Computer users can regularly _____ their existing software.

    4 A company may _____ its competitors' prices.

    5 Governments sometimes _____ the seriousness of a situation.

Adjectives formed with *in*, *off*, *on*, *out* and *over*

Underline the correct alternative.

1 She was momentarily blinded by the headlights of an *incoming/oncoming* **car**.
2 These research findings represent an important contribution to the *ongoing/outgoing* **debate** on the effects of passive smoking.
3 Only 30% of the pupils at this school actually live in the town itself; most children come in by bus from *outdoor/outlying* **areas**.
4 First to arrive on the scene was an *off-duty/off-hand* **police officer**, who had heard the explosion from his kitchen.
5 According to some scientists, humans have only two *inborn/overnight* **fears** – fear of falling and fear of loud noises. All others, it seems, are learned.

Self help

Add the adjective + noun collocations in bold in the above exercise to your vocabulary notebook.

Plans

1 The following adjectives and verbs are all collocates of the nouns **plan** or **plans**. One of the items in each group is very different in meaning to the other three. Underline the odd one out.

Example:

| workable | viable | controversial | feasible |

A controversial plan is one which causes public disagreement or disapproval; the other three adjectives are used to describe plans which are likely to succeed.

1	emergency	bold	daring	audacious
2	elaborate	detailed	intricate	devious
3	clever	ingenious	impracticable	brilliant
4	draw up	devise	carry out	conceive
5	scrap	abandon	jettison	put forward
6	shelve	announce	unveil	reveal

2 Complete the gaps with one of the collocates you have underlined in exercise 1 above. If the word required is a verb, write the correct form.

Example:
Fearing they would lose votes over the issue, the government scrapped their *controversial* plan to reintroduce military service.

1 The proposed peace plan is ill-conceived and _____ : it simply will not work.
2 Local authorities have sensibly drawn up _____ plans to be adopted in the event of further flooding.
3 It's a brilliant plan, but rather too _____ for my liking; it might lay me open to accusations of dishonesty.
4 Plans to build a nuclear power plant in the area have been _____ following strong public opposition.
5 They were prevented from _____ their plan to rob the bank after a police patrol spotted their stolen car and arrested them.
6 Management _____ a plan aimed at increasing productivity, but it was immediately rejected by union leaders.

Self help

Add the collocates of **plan** from exercise 1 to your vocabulary notebook.

Computer technology

1 In **A** and **B** below, combine a word on the left with a word on the right to form new items of vocabulary associated with computers or the Internet. For each new item of vocabulary decide whether it should be written as one word or two.

A				**B**			
1	mouse	**a**	top	1	chat	**a**	engine
2	key	**b**	cam	2	home	**b**	board
3	lap	**c**	mat	3	search	**c**	provider
4	disk	**d**	board	4	service	**d**	room
5	web	**e**	drive	5	bulletin	**e**	page

2 Match each item of vocabulary you formed in exercise 1 to one of the definitions below.

    1 a portable computer

    2 camera connected to a computer so that images can be seen on the Internet

    3 an area on the Internet where a number of people can communicate with each other in real time

    4 a place on the Internet where you can read messages from others and leave your own

    5 a program used to help look for information on the Internet

    6 a piece of soft material for moving a computer mouse around on

    7 a company that provides customers with a connection to the Internet

    8 the set of keys you operate for typing or putting information into a computer

    9 part of a computer that reads information from or records information onto a disk

    10 the first web page to appear on your screen each time you log on to the Internet

Language focus

 Grammar reference on page 222 of the Coursebook.

Talking about the future

Decide which answer **A, B, C** or **D** best fits each space.

1 I hear that Brian and Julie are _____ to start a family soon.

    A projecting   **B** considering   **C** hoping   **D** assuring

2 I _____ they'll accept the offer, but it's worth a try.

    A suspect   **B** hope   **C** doubt   **D** expect

3 I'm just _____ to go out. Can I call you back later?

    A likely   **B** about   **C** almost   **D** soon

4 The company has announced that all employees _____ to receive a special bonus payment at Christmas next year.

    A arrange   **B** go   **C** are   **D** like

5 She's off sick today, but she may _____ be back at work tomorrow.

    A hardly   **B** probably   **C** unlikely   **D** well

6 Come round at 2 o'clock – we should _____ our lunch by then.

    A be finished   **B** have to finish   **C** have finished   **D** have been finishing

7 Building work is _____ to start next month, but I wouldn't be surprised if there was a delay.

    A due   **B** bound   **C** willing   **D** expecting

8 No one else thinks I'll win, but I'm pretty _____ of success myself.

    A definite   **B** confident   **C** assured   **D** doubtless

Determiners

In each of the following sentences there is one grammatical mistake. Correct each mistake by changing or deleting **one** of the words in bold.

Examples: We aren't expecting very ~~much~~ *many* more people to turn up.
We had a ~~very~~ **lot of** problems at work today.

1 I know of **no other any** place which is quite as beautiful as this.

2 I try to go swimming **every another** day during the week – Mondays, Wednesdays and Fridays, usually.

3 **Every a few** months or so we take a day off and go walking in the mountains.

4 We only intended to spend a fortnight there, but we liked it so much we stayed for **other two** weeks.

5 *Determined* is my favourite track on the album but there are **quite a few of** others I like as well.

6 I've been working here for **quite some much** time – nearly ten years, in fact.

7 There's **no much** milk left – enough for breakfast, but that's all.

8 She's had nothing to eat for **some each three** days now – we're getting a bit worried.

English in Use

CAE Part 2

Open cloze

For questions **1–15**, complete the following article by writing **one** word in each space. The exercise begins with an example **(0)**.

Mobile phone throwing Championships

The Mobile Phone Throwing World Championships **(0)** *are* held every year in Finland, the birthplace of the first mobile phone, which was more **(1)** _____ size of a small briefcase than the tiny accessories **(2)** _____ today. When the championships first took place in 2000 there were **(3)** _____ mere 30 competitors, but now the championship attracts well **(4)** _____ 100 people from around the world, all of **(5)** _____ boiling over with frustration at one of the past century's most influential inventions.

The competition is divided **(6)** _____ two sections, contested by teams and individuals. The original category is judged simply on length of throw, but in the freestyle event competitors win on points awarded **(7)** _____ notable performances during the run-up. **(8)** _____ some competitors use their own handsets, most betray a grudging dependence on their phone **(9)** _____ selecting a missile from a large range of second-hand phones **(10)** _____ are supplied by the organizers.

The competition was founded by local businesswoman Christina Lund, inspired by her observations of a country tied to **(11)** _____ mobiles. "I saw that all of **(12)** _____ have very different emotions about our mobiles: much of the time they cause tension and frustration, especially when they get dropped. They never ring when they are supposed **(13)** _____ and they go off **(14)** _____ inconvenient times. So I had the idea of a competition based **(15)** _____ releasing some of that tension."

Gapped text

For questions **1–6**, read the following text and then choose from the list **(A–I)** the best phrase given below it to fill each of the spaces. Each correct phrase may only be used once. Some of the suggested phrases do not fit at all.

Techno-explorers

Not so long ago, explorers **(1)** _____ with the outside world for weeks or months on end. Those days are now gone. Satellite phones, laptops, internet links and GPS navigation aids are common accessories to the modern-day adventurer. Instead of being out of touch for long periods, the explorer **(2)** _____ on which he or she announces to the world their movements, virtually as and when they happen.

These communications are still somewhat restricted by the fact that a satellite dish must be linked from a stationary point, such as base camp. But it **(3)** _____ , such as gyroscopes that can lock into a moving point, enable techno-explorers to send a video datastream of themselves directly onto the Internet via satellite while on the move, so that we, in turn, can witness every step of their adventure in real time.

Is this a good or bad thing? Some claim it detracts from the pure spirit of exploration. Before the 20th century, voyagers **(4)** _____ before anybody heard of their exploits. Undistracted by the everyday world back home, they **(5)** _____ totally immersed in the spirit of adventure. But now, much of an explorer's time is taken up with sending messages out to the world.

According to mountaineer Sir Chris Bonnington, the advantage of running your own website on an expedition is that you have total control over how your story is broadcast. "You're not going through the filter of a newspaper or magazine, you're writing exactly what you want to write" he says. There is an important disadvantage, however. Until recently, for an explorer's family back home, no news was generally perceived to be good news. Now, no news **(6)** _____ as an indication that something has gone wrong.

A will lead others to think of technology

B would usually get in touch

C will probably have a website

D would spend the whole expedition

E won't be long before new developments

F would be gone for years

G will never be as efficient as inventions

H would have no contact

I will most probably be taken

Writing

Formal letter and note

Read the following Writing Part 1 task.

You are a regular user of the main library at the university where you are studying in Britain. You are finding it extremely difficult to concentrate and study in the library, where you feel that facilities are not entirely adequate and regulations are not properly enforced.

Read the letter from your friend below, and the extract from the library regulations, on which you have made some notes. Then, using the information appropriately, write:

a a **letter** to the Library Director informing him/her of the reasons why you find it difficult to study in the library and urging him/her to take action (approximately 200 words);

b a **note** to your friend telling her about the letter you have written and asking to borrow her laptop. You should offer her reassurances that you will take care of it. (approximately 50 words).

You should use your own words as far as possible.

Sorry to hear you're getting a bit stressed out before your exams. It doesn't help at all that you can't get any work done in the library — sounds as if it's really noisy in there. If the library staff don't bother to do anything, the best thing to do is write to the Library Director and see if that gets you anywhere. After all, it's his or her job to see that the regulations are enforced.

In the meantime, if there's anything I can do to help, just let me know.

Best wishes   Kate

UNIVERSITY LIBRARY REGULATIONS

why no specific regulations for mobile phones?

Conduct within the library

- <u>Silence</u> must be maintained in all study areas of the library. Any user disturbed by a failure to observe this or any other regulation should <u>inform a member of staff</u>.   *they never do anything*

- Users may not listen to music of any nature on the library premises. <u>The playing of personal stereos</u> or similar devices with headphones is not allowed.

- Eating, drinking and smoking are forbidden, except in <u>the areas specifically designated</u> for these activities.   *right next to study areas*

Student computing facilities

not enough — never free

- The library provides <u>55 PCs</u> for use by registered students. Each student is allocated 50 megabytes of storage space for saving work and Internet access is free. The computers are intended exclusively for study purposes and <u>the playing of games</u> is prohibited.   *goes on all the time*

- There are 30 positions with network connections for students with computer laptops. Laptops are used entirely at the user's own risk. The library cannot be held responsible for the safety and security of the equipment.

Before you write

Read the following pages in the Coursebook.
Formal letters: pages 193 to196 in Ready for Writing.
Notes: pages 68 and 69 in Unit 5.

9 Going places

Reading

CAE Part 1

Multiple matching

For questions **1–13**, answer by choosing from the reviewers (**A–D**). Some of the choices may be required more than once.

Which reviewer...?

praises the way the writer reveals the truth about the places that are visited	**1** ___
suggests that the impact of the book on readers may be different from what was intended	**2** ___
implies that the writer actually enjoys being involved in dangerous situations	**3** ___
praises the writer for the detailed research that went into the book	**4** ___
implies that the writer is not performing to their best standard in this book	**5** ___
mentions a common misconception that people are often under	**6** ___
appreciates the writer's use of self-mocking humour as a way of creating interest	**7** ___
mentions the writer's determination that lead to the fulfilment of an ambition	**8** ___
alludes to the fact that the writer seems to appreciate adventure more in retrospect	**9** ___
comments that the book can be both fascinating and disturbing to readers	**10** ___
suggests that the writer aims to come across as inexperienced and incapable	**11** ___
praises the writer's perceptive comments regarding issues of the time	**12** ___
suggests that the writer's work has deserved more attention than that of another	**13** ___

Reviews
Geographical's selection of this month's new releases

A *Full Tilt: from Dublin to Delhi with a bicycle*
by Dervla Murphy
Reviewer: James Herron

What first strikes you about Dervla Murphy is her perseverance. On her tenth birthday, she received a bicycle and an atlas and decided there and then that one day she would cycle to India. Unlike most childhood aspirations, this was no passing whim. Twenty one years later, she climbed onto her beloved bike *Roz* and started pedalling for Delhi. Most travel stories contain an element of hardship, but her arduous journey sees her attacked by wolves on the road to Belgrade, swept away by floods in Bulgaria and almost buried by a snowstorm in the Turkish mountains. Nevertheless, the only thing that genuinely set her heart pounding was Roz's brutal treatment at the hands of a hammer-wielding Persian repairman. Her travels through Central Asia occurred in an era far less troubled than ours, but her observations of the first stirrings of political unrest are particularly insightful and prescient. Still, it's her loving description of the rich culture, welcoming people and awe-inspiring landscapes of the terrains she crosses that really sticks in the mind. Murphy may have meant it to read like an epic and amusing fairytale; today however, it seems a sad lament for certain countries that have been ruined by war.

B *Hold the enlightenment* by Tim Cahill
Reviewer: Geordie Torr

While the world has been going crazy over Bill Bryson's acerbic travel tales, his countryman Tim Cahill has been quietly going about his business filing witty stories from the far corners of the globe, and has, I feel, been neglected by the reading public. But where Bryson writes about a rather mundane sort of travel, Cahill – a founding editor and long-time contributor to adventure-travel magazine *Outside*, where many of the pieces in this collection first appeared – seems at his happiest risking life and limb in a distant land. Having said that, Cahill makes it apparent that "Challenging experiences need time to ferment, and an adventure is simply physical and emotional discomfort recollected in tranquillity." And he should know, having faced bandits in the Sahara and sharks in South Africa. These aren't all travel pieces, but the stories share a common thread of wry observation. The laugh-out-loud moments may not be as common or acute as they are in some of his previous features, but *Hold the Enlightenment* is still a highly entertaining introduction to Cahill's work.

C *Surviving extremes* by Nick Middleton
Reviewer: David Mitchell

Nick Middleton is no stranger to severe environments. The quest on this, his latest expedition, was to understand how and why the indigenous people of four extreme habitats manage to survive. His chosen locations were the frozen seas of Greenland, the dense tropical rainforest of the Congo, the arid sun-bleached dunes of Niger's share of the Sahara and Papua New Guinea's near-impenetrable swamps. Despite being a well-travelled geographer and widely respected academic, Middleton still manages to convince you that he is constantly out of his depth. At the same time however, he never shies away from a challenge, whether it involves hunting crocodiles or racing camels. His colourful descriptions of the locations he visits may bring them to life, but at the same time he strips away any picture-postcard illusions so you see the harsh realities for yourself. The resulting book combines Middleton's obvious amazement at the tenacity of the groups he visits with an assortment of characters from whale hunters to desert nomads. He rarely misses an opportunity to laugh at his own 'ineptitude' and this with the genuine apprehension he expresses at the situations he finds himself in make this true adventure story very engaging.

D *Over the edge of the world* by Laurence Bergreen
Reviewer: Jo Sargent

Ferdinand Magellan's desire to discover a route to the Spice Islands meant so much to him that he forsook Portugal, his country and sailed in the service of Spain. This was a betrayal of the highest order, but also an example of his tenacity, a character trait that would ultimately lead to his death. While most people would instantly name Magellan as the first man to circumnavigate the globe, he actually died in the process and that accolade should really belong to his crew. Of the 260 men who sailed forth for fortune and glory, only 18 returned some three years later, a clear illustration of the trials they endured. The scale of their accomplishment becomes all the more apparent as Bergreen lists the failed attempts to copy their journey. Using crew logs and diaries, Bergreen has captured the essence of their journey. His book is an admirably thorough investigation, and historically scrupulous, so there is no need for impassioned language as the bare facts alone keep the reader enthralled. Graphic descriptions of scurvy and torture peppered with mutinies and the threat of the elements provide a thoroughly gripping, if occasionally unsavoury read.

Vocabulary

Wordlist on page 213 of the Coursebook.

Doing things alone

Match each sentence beginning **1–8** with an appropriate ending **a–h**.

1 Media tycoon Wilson McShane is the archetypal **self-made**

2 With nearly 5,000 head of cattle, the island is **self-sufficient**

3 We read about the nautical achievements of **single-handed**

4 The ex-vocalist with *The Recluses* has released her first **solo**

5 At a table in the far corner of the empty pub sat the **solitary**

6 KTL Airlines charge a forty-pound fee for **unaccompanied**

7 The star is too far away to be clearly visible to the **unaided**

8 The railway was built to serve the area's numerous **isolated**

a **children** travelling on all international and domestic flights.

b **figure** of Ed Glen, sipping at his regular Monday morning pint of bitter.

c **millionaire**, who started out as tea boy in the company he now owns.

d **album**, containing cover versions of great jazz songs from the fifties.

e **communities**, at a time when the horse was the only other form of transport.

f **yachtswoman** Ellen MacArthur in Unit 1 of the Coursebook.

g **in milk production**, and is able to export cheese to the mainland.

h **eye**, so a good telescope or pair of binoculars is recommended.

Self help

Study the collocations in bold in the exercise above for one minute. Then cover the sentence endings a–h and look only at the beginnings 1–8. How many collocations can you remember?

Criticism

1 The following adjectives and verbs are all collocates of the nouns *criticism*. Underline the item in each group which does not express a similar meaning to the word(s) in bold. There is an example at the beginning **(0)**.

0 **increasing**	1 **a lot of**	2 **strong**	3 **not affected by**
<u>damaging</u>	considerable	fierce	impervious to
growing	constructive	severe	unmoved by
mounting	widespread	valid	upset by

4 **give**	5 **encounter**	6 **deal successfully with**
arouse	come in for	draw
express	meet with	overcome
voice	respond to	withstand

2 Choose the correct option **A, B, C** or **D**.

1 Her _____ criticism of his work, which was based purely on her intense dislike of him, served only to undermine his self-confidence.
   A fierce   **B** valid   **C** constructive   **D** widespread

2 The President remained _____ by mounting criticism of his leadership and pressed ahead regardless with his controversial programme of policies.
   A upset   **B** unmoved   **C** impervious   **D** overcome

3 Police chiefs yesterday _____ strong criticism of a judge's decision to give a man convicted of armed robbery a six-month suspended sentence.
   A attracted   **B** met with   **C** aroused   **D** voiced

4 The decision to site the nuclear power station next to the nature reserve _____ widespread criticism from opposition politicians and environmental groups.
   A came in   **B** responded to   **C** drew   **D** expressed

Word formation

1 Write the correct form of the word in capitals on the right so that it collocates with each word or words in the group on the left. There is an example at the beginning **(0)**.

0	quality			3	role	
timeless	appeal	**TIME**		_____	evidence	**SUPPORT**
	classic				actress	

1	maintain		
	lose your	_____	**COMPOSE**
	regain		

4	show proof of		
	reveal someone's	_____	**IDENTIFY**
	a case of mistaken		

2	cause considerable		
	suffer great	_____	**HARD**
	overcome economic		

5	competition		
	winning	_____	**ENTER**
	dictionary		

2 Complete each of the gaps with one of the collocations from exercise 1. You may need to change some of the words. There is an example at the beginning **(0)**.

0 Many of Disney's early films are _timeless classics_ , which continue to be enjoyed even now in the modern computer age.

1 A photograph of the _____ in this year's *Inventor of the Future* competition will be printed in the April edition of *Science Today* magazine.

2 Catherine Zeta-Jones won an Oscar for Best _____ for her role in the film *Chicago*.

3 Joseph Rendell was arrested in what seems to have been _____ ; police are still looking for a Joseph Randall in connection with the robbery.

4 He was visibly shocked at the news; it was a while before he _____ and was calm enough to ask how it had happened.

5 The dramatic increase in house prices and rents has _____ to those on low incomes.

Language focus

 Grammar reference on page 223 of the Coursebook.

Creating emphasis

In each of the following sentences there is a word which should not be there. Cross out the word. There is an example at the beginning **(0)**.

0 What annoys me so much about her is the fact ~~of~~ that she never helps with the washing up.

1 It was just after we arrived at the hotel that we have received a call from our neighbour telling us we'd been burgled.

2 I used to hate going to visit my grandparents: all what we ever did was watch television and listen to my grandad talking about politics.

3 It might have been because Jane that rang when I was in the shower – she's the only person I know who'd phone so early in the day.

4 It's not so much what she says that annoys me, and it's more the way she says it.

5 He realized he had little hope of finding his way out of the forest in the fog, so what he did it was to build himself a shelter out of branches and leaves.

6 It was only when the police came at 3 o'clock in the morning so that they finally turned their music down.

English in Use

Multiple-choice cloze

For questions **1–15**, read the text below and then decide which answer **A, B, C** or **D** best fits each space. The exercise begins with an example **(0)**.

Lost luggage

You get off your plane and **(0)** _____ your way to the Baggage Reclaim area, where you **(1)** _____ the carousel for your flight and wait patiently for your luggage. After quite some time spent waiting, there is no **(2)** _____ of your bags and you begin to consider the possibility that they may have gone **(3)** _____ . What should you do?

Firstly, don't panic. The most likely **(4)** _____ is that your bags **(5)** _____ didn't make it onto the flight, perhaps because they were mislaid at the departure airport, or perhaps because the aircraft had already **(6)** _____ its weight allowance. If they **(7)** _____ to appear on the carousel, report the loss before you leave the baggage hall and go through customs. **(8)** _____ your luggage should be no problem, provided you've kept **(9)** _____ of

your baggage checks – those little barcodes stuck to the back of your tickets at check-in.

Go to the handling agent's desk and **(10)** _____ a Property Irregularity Report (PIR) form, which describes the checked bag and its **(11)** _____ . Make **(12)** _____ you mention all items of value, because if the bag is never found, your insurance company may compare the articles on your claim form with those on the PIR. Then, ask the baggage-services manager for a contact telephone number and confirm that your bags will be forwarded to your final **(13)** _____ .

Most bags **(14)** _____ up within a day or two, but if yours never show (and it may be weeks before the airline accepts that they are permanently lost), you can claim **(15)** _____ from the airline.

0	**A** go	**B** get	**C** <u>make</u>	**D** walk
1	**A** locate	**B** place	**C** position	**D** situate
2	**A** indication	**B** sign	**C** notice	**D** mark
3	**A** lost	**B** missing	**C** absent	**D** misplaced
4	**A** example	**B** understanding	**C** clarification	**D** explanation
5	**A** simply	**B** easily	**C** only	**D** cleanly
6	**A** surpassed	**B** overtaken	**C** exceeded	**D** outdone
7	**A** lack	**B** omit	**C** avoid	**D** fail
8	**A** Retracing	**B** Retaining	**C** Recovering	**D** Reinstating
9	**A** control	**B** hold	**C** property	**D** hand
10	**A** carry out	**B** complete	**C** fulfil	**D** realize
11	**A** contents	**B** inside	**C** filling	**D** packing
12	**A** safe	**B** clear	**C** confident	**D** sure
13	**A** destiny	**B** destination	**C** termination	**D** terminus
14	**A** come	**B** turn	**C** bring	**D** put
15	**A** refund	**B** reparation	**C** amendment	**D** compensation

(**CAE Part 5**) **Register transfer**

For questions **1–13**, read the following note from the manager of a tour company to his secretary and use the information in it to complete the numbered gaps in the advertising leaflet. The words you need **do not occur** in the letter from the form teacher. **Use no more than two words in each gap**. The exercise begins with an example **(0)**.

NOTE

Paula

Here's the information for the leaflet:

- There are combination train and coach tours to see the north of England every other Saturday during the summer.
- Point out that it's a chance to go to many different places it wouldn't normally be possible to see all in one day. Give them an idea of the type of place we take them to and tell them they won't feel let down.
- We book them a seat on an InterCity train and put them on a luxury air-conditioned coach for the tour itself – all very comfortable.
- Tours set off from London King's Cross station. Tell them to get to the station on time – the train won't wait for them.

Prices

- Tell them what they get for their money – the train and coach journeys, the information pack and an experienced guide.
- Reduced rates apply to students – as long as they've got an *International Student Card* – and kids under 14 and retired people pay half-price.

Payment

- They have to pay a deposit of 40% a week before if they want to make sure of a place.
- If for any reason we have to call off a tour, we'll let them know at least three days before they're due to leave and give them <u>all</u> their deposit back.

Northern Railroad Tours

See the north of England by both train and coach with Northern Railroad Tours – available on (0) *alternate* **Saturdays throughout the summer.**

Our tours offer you the **(1)** _____ to visit a wide **(2)** _____ different places you would not normally be able to see in just one day. Whether it's a coastal fishing village, an imposing castle or some picturesque scenery, you won't be **(3)** _____ . To guarantee your comfort we make a seat **(4)** _____ you on an InterCity train and provide you with a luxury air-conditioned coach for the actual tour.

All tours start from London King's Cross station. Clients are advised to arrive **(5)** _____ the station as trains will leave at the stated time.

Prices

Prices quoted **(6)** _____ all travel by rail and coach, an information pack and an experienced guide. **(7)** _____ available to students, **(8)** _____ that they hold an *International Student Card*. Children under 14 and **(9)** _____ pay half-price.

Payment

A deposit of 40% is payable a week in **(10)** _____ in order to ensure a place. Should for any reason a tour have to **(11)** _____ , clients will be notified at least three days before the scheduled date of **(12)** _____ and given a **(13)** _____ of the deposit paid.

Writing

CAE Part 1

Report

1 Read the following Writing Part 1 task.

You are studying at a language school in Brighton in the south of England. You are the secretary of the Student Committee, and the Social and Cultural Programme Organizer has asked you to write a report providing feedback on the activities organized during the Autumn term.

Read the memo from the Programme Organizer, the copy of the Autumn Term Programme, on which you have made some notes, together with comments from five other students. Then, **using the information appropriately**, write the report as instructed by the Programme Organizer in her memo.

Memo

To: **Secretary of Student Committee**
From: **Elisa Burrows,** Social and Cultural Programme Organizer
Re: **Autumn Term Programme**

I am currently organizing the social and cultural programme for the Winter term, which runs from January to March. To enable me to do this effectively, I need to have some idea of how students felt about this term's activities. I would like to know, therefore:

• what students think of the programme as a whole
• some of the main positive and negative aspects of the programme
• what improvements could be made in the Winter term.

As well as giving me your own thoughts, could you get some feedback from other students and then write me a report covering the three points above?

Brighton Language School

Social and Cultural Programme

Autumn term

An integral part of the English Language learning experience at Brighton Language School is the Social and Cultural Programme, which provides the opportunity to practise your English in a variety of contexts.

Social events

The perfect way to relax, have fun and meet students from other classes. Don't miss the regular:

great fun —
• karaoke evenings
a bit cold! —
• discos, beach parties and barbecues
• film nights
• badminton, tennis and squash tournaments

Cultural events

mine didn't know very much —
With your teacher as personal guide, our wide range of activities enable you to experience the culture of the country, both present and past. Most
no they aren't! —
of the talks and trips are free or at discount prices. They include:
very interesting —
• museum and art gallery visits to London
• theatre and concert trips
• day excursions to areas of outstanding historical interest
we didn't do much discussing —
• lecture talks and discussions on literary, political, sociological and cultural topics

Weekend excursions

too far —
See more of the country on our weekend excursions by coach to places such as Bath, Edinburgh, York and the Lake District.

I enjoyed the social events. The film nights were a bit of a waste of time, though – we just watched a DVD, and that was it.

The weekend excursions were the best part. It was just a shame it took so long to get to all the places.

The social events were good fun, but how about more team sports?

Some of the lecture talks were a bit boring – 2 hours just listening to someone isn't very educational.

Some of the cultural trips and excursions were quite pricey. I couldn't afford to go on many – a pity, because they looked really interesting.

2   Decide whether the following statements are true (T) or false (F).

Content

1   The task requires you to include all the positive and negative aspects of the programme, as mentioned in your own notes and the comments of the five other students.

Organization and cohesion

2 Either of the following two plans would be acceptable.

Plan A	**Plan B**
Introduction	Introduction
Students' overall opinion of the programme	Students' overall opinion of the programme
Social events: positive & negative aspect(s)	Positive aspects
Cultural events: positive & negative aspect(s)	Negative aspects
Weekend excursions: positive & negative aspect(s)	Recommendations
Recommendations	

3 An overall heading and individual paragraph headings are completely unnecessary.

Range of language

4 The language of recommendation would be useful here.

Target reader and register

5 The register will depend on your interpretation of your relationship with the Programme Organizer, but it must be consistent.

3   Write your report in approximately 250 words. You should use your own words as far as possible.

Don't forget!

- Where possible, organize your own and other students' comments into logical groups or pairs.
  eg *no they aren't!* together with *Some of the cultural trips and excursions were quite pricey.*
- Base your suggestions for improvements on these comments.
  eg *organize cheaper cultural events*

Reading

Multiple matching

1 Read the magazine article on four teachers with flat-sharing experiences. For questions **1–16**, answer by choosing from the teachers **A–D**. Some of the choices may be required more than once.

Of which teacher are the following statements true?

I might look for a flatmate in the right circumstances.	1 ___
Finding a flatmate now would represent a backward step to me.	2 ___
I suspect my flatmate considered my behaviour to be odd.	3 ___
I feel that it is necessary to compromise at the moment.	4 ___
Talking about housework duties eventually proved to be pointless.	5 ___
There were no restrictions on my freedom in that situation.	6 ___
I did not feel obliged to help out much with the housework.	7 ___
I would feel guilty if I did not make a proper contribution.	8 ___
I recommend that people who are considering living together are honest with each other.	9 ___
It became necessary to have a frank discussion about housework.	10 ___
It was important to us that the flat was easily affordable.	11 ___
Sharing a flat can be successful as long as the flatmates have something in common.	12 ___
I was less comfortable after others in the house began to depend on me financially.	13 ___
Setting up in a flat was not as easy as I had expected.	14 ___
My flatmate's hard work in the flat made up for a personality flaw.	15 ___
I felt obliged to keep quiet about behaviour I disapproved of.	16 ___

Two's company, three's a crowd?

Flat-sharing has long been a tradition in New Zealand, and not just for students. But while there are those who love the sense of communal living, there are others who can't wait to establish their own private nest. Lisa Simpson speaks to four teachers.

A Craig Chambers

A born and bred New Zealander, and now house owner, Craig has had his share of flat-sharing experiences. According to him, the whole process of finding a flat can be reasonably relaxing. More importantly, provided flatmates' backgrounds are similar and their interests compatible, there's no reason why it all shouldn't work out well. 'It may not be easy, but potential flatmates need to be upfront with one another and establish what living arrangements everyone will find acceptable. Pretending that something's OK is likely to cause serious problems later.' He's speaking from experience. Craig once found himself flat-sharing in Rome while teaching for a language school. 'The other tenant, an English man, was also working for them. The big issue was that he was totally uninterested in cleaning. Despite a great many hints, he never picked up on them, and would often come home and comment that the cleaning had been done, but not do anything himself. No doubt he thought I was obsessive.' Craig felt it necessary to put up with the situation as their contract with the school had six months to run and any confrontation would have ultimately created greater tension. Perhaps it was this experience that led Craig to buying his first house shortly after. 'I can't imagine ever being in that sort of flatting situation again. I realize it's cheaper but I prefer my privacy and independence and I'm not prepared to give those up.'

B Derene Els

Having emigrated to New Zealand from South Africa four years ago, Derene is currently living with four members of her family 'I pay a boarding fee as in any other flat share situation. I know some people might find that strange, but I do it out of a sense of responsibility. It wouldn't be right not to, especially as I'm working.' She feels that she has her own privacy to a certain extent but: 'I have to share the living area with everybody which means taking turns with the television remote control for a start. I just have to accept that while we're all still living under the same roof.' Derene is currently keeping an eye out for a small apartment. Her criteria is simply 'near the coast' as she grew up on a farm and needs a sense of open space around her. Perhaps this is what drew her to Australia where she took time off from her job in New Zealand to work as a translator during the Sydney Olympics. After that contract came to an end, she decided to stay on with the host family who'd been putting her up. 'Once the arrangement became more formal, when I felt they were relying on me for income, I was not so at ease,' she explains. 'But I still felt obliged to be sociable and didn't want to appear rude by keeping myself to myself. All the same, I could still come and go as I wished.'

C Sarah Nuttall

Originally from the UK, Sarah has spent the last five years in New Zealand. She's found the local flatting experience rather different to what she was used to. 'There aren't so many flats available here,' she explains. 'As well as this, in London the flats are usually fully furnished whereas in New Zealand you only get a cooker. When my boyfriend and I first got here, it had never occurred to us that we would have to go out and buy loads of second hand stuff just to get started.' She's adamant that there's no room for a third person in her flat. 'We've talked about getting an extra person in to reduce costs, but our privacy comes first. But if I were ever single again, I suppose I'd consider it. It would be a good way of meeting friends.' Sarah's first flatting experience was in London with four friends she'd been to university with. She admits that there were both good and bad times. 'We hardly ever argued at first, except for minor quarrels over the washing up. Eventually however, things came to a head when the kitchen became unusable. 'We thought that we should be more responsible at our age. We had a group meeting and the rules were laid down. They were effective for about three weeks and then things went back to the way they were.'

D Patrick Franks

Now in the complicated process of looking for his own house, Patrick spent his second year of university flatting with three other students. There was a unanimous decision that the accommodation had to be within their student means and in close proximity to the university. Getting along with the others did not prove to be much of a problem. 'There were no real disputes. One woman, Cathy, was extremely talkative, so much so that you'd end up not listening. But she was generous and she very much pulled her weight around the flat so we could live with that.' He confesses to little participation when it came to housework. 'There were times when we'd all pitch in, but the problem was that both my best friend and I spent a lot of time away from the flat. It was agreed that we weren't as responsible for the messes created and I wasn't going to argue with that.' When that flat got sold, he found the easiest option was to move in with his brother. 'I can't say I had that much in common with him. We took care of ourselves and we'd occasionally go to movies together.' And now the flat-sharing seems to be coming to an end? 'I couldn't imagine flatting ever again. Living with a stranger would mean I'd failed in some way, like I was de-maturing.'

2 Complete the gaps with the correct form of one of the expressions in the box. All the expressions appeared in the reading text.

come to	come to an end	come to a head	come first	come and go

1 Of course my work is important, but my family always _____ .

2 I can do the ironing or clean the house, but when it _____ cooking, I'm absolutely useless.

3 Tensions had been steadily increasing, and things _____ last week when riots broke out and the government was forced to act.

4 Her parents have given her a key, so she can _____ as she pleases.

5 You can see that summer is _____ ; the leaves have started falling off the trees already.

Vocabulary

Wordlist on page 214 of the Coursebook.

1 In **A** and **B** complete each gap with one of the words from the boxes.

A

| bee | dog | owl | lion | mouse |

1 I was woken up at two o'clock by an inconsiderate _____ **hooting** monotonously in the tree next to my tent.

2 We heard the **squeaking** of a _____ coming from the cupboard where we had set the trap.

3 A honey _____ came **buzzing** past, a sign that spring had at last arrived.

4 The neighbours' _____ spends the day **whining** and scratching at the door while they're both out at work.

5 What's the name of the company that has that _____ **roaring** before the beginning of each film?

B

| leaves | floorboards | stomach | drum | music |

1 His _____ **rumbled**, reminding him that he hadn't eaten since lunchtime.

2 The _____ **rustled** in the gentle breeze.

3 I wish that child would stop **banging** that _____ !

4 *You* can't complain – you have your _____ **blaring out** all day.

5 We heard voices and the sound of footsteps on **creaking** _____ .

2 Choose the correct answer **A**, **B**, **C** or **D**.

1 He's a very well-behaved little boy – I rarely have to _____ my voice to him.
  A shout   **B** lose   **C** raise   **D** lift

2 As we climbed higher, the noise of the traffic gradually _____ away.
  A faded   **B** left   **C** grew   **D** weakened

3 I couldn't hear what they were saying; they were in the next room so their voices were _____ .
  A booming   **B** muffled   **C** hoarse   **D** rough

4 She came in, picked up her things, and left before I could _____ a sound.
  A pronounce **B** tell   **C** express   **D** utter

5 There was a _____ party going on next door last night; the police eventually came at half past one and put a stop to it.
  A constant   **B** continuous **C** roomy   **D** rowdy

6 He proposed to her in the _____ lit restaurant of the hotel with piano music playing in the background.
  A soundly   **B** softly   **C** smoothly   **D** sparsely

7 Cleaners worked overtime to get the place looking spick and _____ for the presidential visit.
  A spam   **B** spot   **C** spin   **D** span

8 Factory workers lived in council flats which were _____ built and badly maintained.
  A poorly   **B** weakly   **C** highly   **D** slightly

9 Immigrants live in _____ conditions, with up to 15 sharing a small room.
  A spacious   **B** cramped   **C** restrained **D** constrained

10 The town is ideally _____ for visiting both London and the south coast.
  A set   **B** centred   **C** orientated **D** situated

Language focus

 Grammar reference on page 223 of the Coursebook.

Participle clauses

Combine the following pairs of sentences using participle clauses.

Examples:
Sheffield FC was founded in 1857. This makes it the oldest football club in the world.
Sheffield FC was founded in 1857, making it the oldest football club in the world.

He inherited a huge sum of money from his grandmother. He decided to give up work.
Having inherited a huge sum of money from his grandmother, he decided to give up work.

1 'Lord of the Rings: Return of the King' won 11 Oscars. It equalled the record held by 'Ben Hur' and 'Titanic' for the highest number of Academy Awards.

2 We finally discovered where the leak was. We called in a plumber.

3 The school now has 1,254 students. This represents a 6% increase on last year's figure.

4 Part of the stadium roof collapsed. It injured six spectators.

5 I am not a parent. I can take my holidays whenever I like.

6 The team has had a disastrous season so far. It has won only three of its last sixteen games.

7 Our parents went away for the weekend. My brother and I had a party.

8 I was walking home from school yesterday. I bumped into Alex.

English in Use

CAE Part 3

Error correction

In **most** lines of the following text there is **one** unnecessary word. It is **either** grammatically incorrect **or** does not fit in with the sense of the text. If a line is correct, put a tick (✓) in the space at the end of the line. If a line has an unnecessary word, write the word in the space. The exercise begins with two examples **(0)** and **(00)**.

DIY dreamer doubles his money

0	Four years ago John Felton realized why a long-held ambition to	*why*
00	build his own home in Merseyside. Now he is reaping the rewards:	✓
1	the house has also doubled in value. While it cost around £300,000	
2	to build, including the land, it is now on the market for £700,000. If	
3	the living rooms are on the first floor, around a glass-walled atrium,	
4	with those large windows offering views over the Dee estuary. Four	
5	bedrooms occupy on the ground floor and a detached garage acts as	
6	a gym. "In my job I've built offices, schools and commercial premises,	
7	but I always wanted to build my own house. Five years ago, I found	
8	out a plot and came up with a simple design. The architect modified it	
9	and produced a home that I'm immensely proud of it," says Felton.	
10	"It took more a year to build and I hand-picked the craftsmen. But like	
11	most self-build projects it went well over budget. If only the choice	
12	was between money and getting the best of, I opted for the latter,"	
13	admits Felton, who lives with his wife, Bernadette, and another	
14	stepdaughter, Laura. Now that he is selling to fulfil his next dream,	
15	to build a bigger and much better house for his family. "I should soon	
16	have started doing this years ago. It's satisfying and profitable," he says.	

(**CAE Part 1**)   **Multiple-choice cloze**

For questions **1–15**, read the text below and then decide which answer **A, B, C** or **D** best fits each space. The exercise begins with an example **(0)**.

Flat to Let

Location: Norfolk Gardens, Westgate

No. of bedrooms: 1

Price per week: £420

This large one-bedroomed flat, situated in the **(0)** _____ residential suburb of Westgate and **(1)** _____ the nearby St John's Park, is ideal for a busy single person or couple. The accommodation is **(2)** _____ located in the heart of the suburb within **(3)** _____ walking distance of the wide range of amenities **(4)** _____ by both Westgate and the fashionable Donatello Road Market.

(5) _____ decorated and carpeted, the property **(6)** _____ a double bedroom, good-sized reception room, large living room, **(7)** _____ fitted kitchen and a bathroom with quality shower. Tenants also have **(8)** _____ of their own secure underground parking **(9)** _____ . The flat is simply but **(10)** _____ furnished and the south-facing living room is pleasantly light and **(11)** _____ , with large picture windows which offer superb views of the surrounding **(12)** _____ .

What **(13)** _____ this property apart from other accommodation with similar **(14)** _____ is its very acceptable price, given its central location and excellent transport links to other parts of the city. For **(15)** _____ details or to arrange a viewing telephone 020 786 50990.

0 A greenish	**B** leafy	**C** flowering	**D** blooming
1 A overseeing	**B** overhanging	**C** overlooking	**D** overreaching
2 A appropriately	**B** fittingly	**C** suitably	**D** conveniently
3 A easy	**B** simple	**C** close	**D** nearby
4 A offered	**B** proposed	**C** given	**D** produced
5 A Newly	**B** Lately	**C** Ultimately	**D** Proximately
6 A composes	**B** comprises	**C** comprehends	**D** compounds
7 A absolutely	**B** extremely	**C** fully	**D** entirely
8 A service	**B** employment	**C** application	**D** use
9 A permit	**B** ticket	**C** room	**D** space
10 A sparsely	**B** plainly	**C** richly	**D** tastefully
11 A draughty	**B** breezy	**C** airy	**D** gusty
12 A part	**B** area	**C** sector	**D** zone
13 A sets	**B** puts	**C** keeps	**D** holds
14 A types	**B** kinds	**C** characteristics	**D** aspects
15 A added	**B** advanced	**C** further	**D** larger

CAE Part 4

Word formation

For questions **1–15**, use the words in the boxes to the right of the texts to form **one** word that fits the same numbered space in the text. The exercise begins with an example **(0)**.

Ironing

Many people hate ironing, but is it really such a tedious and **(0)** *disagreeable* chore? When done in the **(1)** _____ and warmth of a cosy kitchen with the radio on, it can be a fairly pleasant way of spending your time. And when it's finished, there's always something rather **(2)** _____ about a pile of neatly ironed clothes.

Anyway, love it or loathe it, here are a few guidelines:

- Before you start, **(3)** _____ you have enough wardrobe space to allow your clothes to hang **(4)** _____ once they have been ironed.
- Plug in the iron close to the ironing board. A length of cord stretched across a room represents a serious **(5)** _____ hazard.
- Read the care label on each garment for the recommended ironing **(6)** _____ and the appropriate temperature **(7)** _____ . If in doubt, start with a cool iron and increase the temperature as necessary.
- Iron clothes while they are still slightly damp.

0	AGREE
1	PRIVATE
2	SATISFY
3	SURE
4	FREE
5	SAFE
6	PROCEED
7	SET

Treehouses

In some of Britain's most exclusive **(8)** _____ , where swimming pools and conservatories are commonplace, the most stylish are opting for the only addition **(9)** _____ to turn the neighbours green – a luxury treehouse for adults. **(10)** _____ more than £20,000, they come with drinks cabinets, dining tables, **(11)** _____ kitchens and balconies. Some owners find their treehouses are perfect for holding **(12)** _____ business meetings, and one businessman liked his so much that he made it into a permanent office. Derek and Edwina Lilley spent £24,000 on Britain's most **(13)** _____ and extravagant treehouse. It took four weeks to build and can accommodate 35 for drinks parties with ease. It has a kitchen **(14)** _____ with a combination oven, grill and hob, as well as hot and cold **(15)** _____ water.

8	NEIGHBOUR
9	GUARANTEE
10	COST
11	FIT
12	INTERRUPT
13	LUXURY
14	EQUIP
15	RUN

Writing

Contribution to a brochure

1 Read the following Writing Part 2 task and the model below.

A brochure is being produced in English aimed at encouraging foreign visitors to spend their holidays in your country. You have been asked to write an entry on the type of accommodation available for those people wishing to enjoy a countryside holiday. You should include information on at least two different types of accommodation, pointing out the positive features of each type and giving a general idea of prices.

Write your **entry** for the brochure.

Countryside Accommodation

If your aim in coming to our country is to get away from it all, the choice of rural accommodation is wide, with something to suit every pocket.

Campsites

In the lower price bracket are the many campsites to be found in some of our most beautiful rural areas. These are generally situated well away from busy towns, guaranteeing peace and quiet and a well earned rest from the hustle and bustle of everyday life. Most cater for children, offering a range of facilities designed to provide weary parents with a welcome break.

Prices vary depending on the campsite and the type of accommodation you choose . A family of four with their own tent in a three-star campsite can pay as little as 300 Euros for a week in the high season. A rather more expensive option is to hire a caravan, which works out at about 90 Euros a night but accommodates up to 6 people.

Rural Houses

If comfort is a major factor when choosing accommodation and money is no object, you could stay at one of the large number of rural houses located throughout the country. These are usually restored country houses or mansions, with all the benefits of a five-star hotel, but always in a peaceful countryside setting. And for those who like to be active on holiday, there are plenty of organized outdoor activities on offer, such as horse riding, hiking, canoeing or even paragliding.

Rural houses are clearly at the upper end of the price range, with a double room costing anywhere between 150 and 300 Euros per night, but if you really want to pamper yourself, there's no better way.

---

2 Underline those sections of the model which are used to talk about the positive features of the accommodation.

   Example: to be found in some of our most beautiful rural areas

3 In the box below write those expressions from the model which refer to price.

   Example: with something to suit every pocket

4 Circle any present and past participles which introduce participle clauses.

   Example: (guaranteeing) *peace and quiet*

5 Write an answer to the following Part 2 task:

   A brochure is being produced in English aimed at encouraging foreign visitors to spend their holidays in your country. You have been asked to write an entry on the type of accommodation available for those people wishing to enjoy a holiday in the city or large town in which you live or which is nearest to your home. You should include information on at least two different types of accommodation, pointing out the positive features of each type and giving a general idea of prices.

   Write your **entry** for the brochure in approximately 250 words.

   ### Don't forget!

   - Plan your answer before you write.
   - Organize your ideas into logical paragraphs. Include a *brief* introduction.
   - Use some of the language from the model when referring to price.
   - Participle clauses add variety to your writing and help create a good impression.

   ### Before you write

   - See page 199 in the Coursebook for more information and useful language for brochures and guidebooks.

The accommodation in the castle is well ventilated and allows you to experience nature at first hand.

11 A cultural education

Reading

Multiple matching

For questions **1–18**, answer by choosing from the people **(A–F)**. You may choose any person more than once.

Of which person is the following true?

He values other people's desire to be creative even if they are not successful.	**1** ____
He describes how a good relationship was established.	**2** ____
He expresses regret that Paris is producing art work which is of average standard.	**3** ____
He mentions a misunderstanding that was eventually resolved.	**4** ____
He states that he has always maintained the same opinion of Paris.	**5** ____
He comments on the importance of maintaining social customs.	**6** ____
He believes that Parisians have strong opinions which they like to express.	**7** ____
He expresses admiration for Parisians' polite behaviour.	**8** ____
He feels that it should be easier for people to walk around Paris.	**9** ____
He expresses regret that he will never belong to a particular group.	**10** ____
He states that he feels more comfortable living in Paris than in his current city.	**11** ____
He feels Paris could be more lively if more people from different cultures lived there.	**12** ____
He admits that he only recently appreciated a certain aspect of Paris.	**13** ____
He comments that it is almost impossible to gain the approval of Parisians for your work.	**14** ____
He mentions a sudden decision which proved to be the right one.	**15** ____
He suggests that French art would benefit from foreign influences.	**16** ____
He appreciates the way in which Paris can improve his mood.	**17** ____
He appreciates the way that people can be spontaneous when it comes to enjoying themselves.	**18** ____

My Paris

It's still the perfect cultural destination. So we asked those on intimate terms with the French capital to tell us what it means to them and to reveal their favourite places.

A *Gilbert Adair:* writer

I lived in Paris in the late 1960s and through the 1970s. Although I've been back in London for the past 20 years or so, I still feel more at home there than I do here. I went native, I suppose. I tend to stay in Montparnasse, and what's curious about it is that even though it's 90 years since artists like Picasso and Modigliani were around, something of their spirit survives. Paris must be the only place where you see people on their own in a café, scribbling in a notepad. I always have the impression that whatever they're writing is probably never going to be any good and won't be published, but that's not the point. However, in a sense, in artistic terms, Paris is going through a rather mediocre period. Maybe it has something to do with attempts by the establishment to keep French art 'pure'; that is to say, not affected by any culture not French. Because of this, Paris has become something of a museum.

B *Andreas Whittam-Smith:* editor

I first went there when I was 20. I thought that it was the most romantic city in the world and my view hasn't changed. I find it beautiful, the architecture particularly, and the way the long streets are always finished off with a building at the end of them. I don't enjoy the fact that it's a city that favours the motorist over the pedestrian, for whom it can be a challenge just to get about, to cross the road even. One of my favourite places in Paris is an emporium called *Deyrolle* on the *Rue du Bac*. They sell all kinds of geological specimens and butterflies. Every time we have people staying with us we take them there and they always buy something.

C *Charles Darwent:* art critic

The launderette by my flat in Belleville sums up Paris for me. You put your clothes in the machine and then, committing the machine's number to memory, you walk to a different machine in a different room and feed it coins. Someone could steal your stuff while this was going on but the beggar lady who lives there would stop them. Though she's barred from the café next door, she put in a good word for me with the owner. She told him the reason I had never greeted him in French on walking in wasn't because I was rude, but English. So he took to crossing the bar whenever I entered, shaking my hand and roaring '*Bonjour, Anglais*' until I gave in and began to pre-empt him. Now we get on famously. Paris is all about following ritual. Everything – how you feed a washing machine, the way you greet someone, the way you enter a bar. There's a cafe near here where the customers spend hours discussing the food. They are pompous and ridiculous and I long to be one of them, and never will.

D *Philippe Starck:* interior designer

Despite being born in Paris, it was only a few years ago that I took a proper look at the city and truly saw its beauty. But it's not about the stone or the architecture; it's the people, the Parisians. The people are highly critical. No matter whether you make something good or bad, it will always be bad – they are very negative, which makes it the hardest place to create something. At the same time, it's their vigilance that creates some of the best quality in the world. It took me six years to discover this secret. Parisians are incredibly snobbish people – they create tribes and stick to them. There's one for music, one for art, one for journalists, and they like to fight each other. We could never just follow a leader – people are too independent-minded and aren't afraid to be frank.

E Douglas Kennedy: writer

In 1998, I was on a book tour, and staying in a hotel. I spent the whole night walking and ended up in the Place de la Concorde at 6am, just in time for sunrise. The whole place was completely deserted and not a car to be seen. I thought to myself, I have to live here – and so I bought a flat in St Germain. It was spontaneous, I suppose, but it turned out very well. You can live a proper urban life in Paris: within five minutes' walk from your door there can be at least 15 cinemas and several excellent markets. No matter how depressed I feel, or how bad the writing is going, the sight of the city makes me feel better. It is much more compact than London, so even though you can never find a cab at night, you can always find your way home. There is, however, not the multi-cultural buzz you get in London: I think this robs the city of a certain dynamism.

F Raymond Blanc: chef

Two and a half years ago, I went with my girlfriend to see *C'est Formidable* at the Moulin Rouge theatre. Afterwards we ate in Montmartre. It was a beautiful, warm evening and there was a very happy atmosphere. At about 1am everybody started singing and dancing. This happens a lot in Paris – one person suddenly begins and then other people join in. When I look at Paris I see the sheer beauty and scale of the architecture. It is a totally amazing place and there is a certain civility about Parisians which I think is wonderful. It is a shame that all the best restaurants in Paris are closed at the weekend. It is also much quieter, than say, London or Barcelona, which have a much younger and more lively culture.

Vocabulary

Wordlist on page 214 of the Coursebook.

Sight

Underline the correct alternative.

1 Icy roads and **poor** *visibility/sight/view* due to fog meant driving conditions were extremely dangerous.

2 I've always **had poor** *eyesight/view/look*, whereas my brother, who's fifty-six, still **has twenty-twenty** *vision/eye/sight* and will probably never have to wear glasses.

3 I'd hate to be a film star, always **in the public** *vision/eye/show*, recognized wherever you go.

4 As soon as I mentioned Sally, Paul **gave me a knowing** *sight/view/look*. 'But Sally and I are just good friends,' I protested.

5 The cliffs were **a welcome** *vision/sight/show* after so many weeks at sea.

6 He suffered a heart attack on stage, **in** *complete/open/full* **view of** the audience.

7 I picked up the shiny stone to **take a** *handier/tighter/closer* **look**.

8 For most of this week the comet will be **visible with the** *naked/bare/open* **eye**.

9 Could you *keep/put/set* **your eye on** my bag, please? I'm just going to the toilet.

10 We scanned the night sky, hoping to *give/catch/gain* **sight of** the comet.

Read and write

1 Complete each of the phrasal verbs with an appropriate word from the box. In each section **1–4** the word required for both spaces is the same.

up	into	off	out

1 I've just **written** _____ **to** the Polish Tourist Office **for** information on the Mazurian Lakes.
Western governments have come under increasing pressure to **write** _____ Third World **debts**.

2 As soon as the interview was over, he **wrote** _____ **his notes** and faxed the report to his boss.
Contract law is a complex area, so it's wise to **read** _____ **on the subject** and take professional advice.

3 She swallowed hard and **wrote** _____ **a cheque for** £4,560.
Let's hear what you've written for number 3. Can you **read** _____ **your answer**, please, Alex?

4 The right to keep and bear arms is **written** _____ **the constitution** of the United States.
It's only an opinion poll – it would be wrong to **read too much** _____ **the results**.

2 Match each pair of definitions **a–d** to the appropriate pair of verbs in bold in exercise 1 above.

a include in (a law, contract or agreement); think something means more than it really does

b record in a full and complete form; read a lot about a subject in order to get information

c apply to an organization asking them to send something; cancel

d complete a printed document (eg prescription, receipt) with information; read aloud

Language focus

 Grammar reference on page 223 of the Coursebook.

Inversion

1 Complete each of the gaps with **one** word.

Statement from the main opposition party

At **(1)** _____ time in the last 60 years **(2)** _____ literacy levels in this country been so low. Not only **(3)** _____ the nation's teenagers reading less than ever before, **(4)** _____ many are also incapable of writing more than one sentence without making a spelling or punctuation mistake. **(5)** _____ since the 1940s have we witnessed such a decline in reading and writing standards.

(6) _____ no circumstances must this situation be permitted to continue. Only **(7)** _____ the government introduces a comprehensive reading programme for three to five-year-olds **(8)** _____ standards improve. **(9)** _____ then will the nation's youth be able to break free from the chains of illiteracy and recover its dignity. **(10)** _____ no account must we allow ourselves to be complacent; action must be taken now.

---

2   Complete each sentence with a suitable phrase. There is an example at the beginning (0).

0 Not for one moment *did we suspect* that David had stolen it – it took us all completely by surprise.

1 No sooner _____ home than my mother phoned.

2 Only when _____ the news on television did she realize the full scale of the tragedy.

3 Never before in all my working life _____ such an incompetent boss.

4 Not until you've tidied your room _____ you to go out and play with your friends!

5 Hardly _____ his new job when the company ran into problems and made him redundant.

6 At no point in the marathon _____ of giving up: I had promised myself I would finish it.

7 Never again _____ her advice – I'm in more trouble now than I was before.

8 Little _____ that someone was recording their conversation.

English in Use

CAE Part 5

Register transfer

For questions **1–13**, read the following advertising leaflet and use the information in it to complete the numbered gaps in the informal letter from a woman to her friend, who is a teacher. The words you need **do not occur** in the advertising leaflet. **Use no more than two words in each gap**. The exercise begins with an example **(0)**.

Visit Rodford Museum of Theatre

Situated in Levisham Street, close to the city centre.

We can provide a great day out for young and old alike. The museum houses several permanent exhibitions of costumes, props, manuscripts and other artefacts, which trace the history of the theatre from the fourteen hundreds to modern times.

We also stage regular productions of classic plays: from May to July of this year a series of works by our most famous of playwrights, William Shakespeare, will be performed in the open air – weather permitting, of course!

There are a number of special activities for groups, including workshops and demonstrations. Children and adults can go backstage at the theatre, try on costumes and even 'tread the boards'.

Admission charges: Entrance to the museum is free.

Opening hours: Monday to Friday 10.00–20.00
Saturday 10.00–18.00
Closed Sundays and Bank Holidays.

A minimum of three weeks' notice is required for those groups wishing to participate in the special activities.

For more information, please consult our website or phone us on 0190 211324.

INFORMAL LETTER

Dear Sven

I've just picked up a leaflet for the Rodford Museum of Theatre, which is not **(0)** <u>far from</u> the city centre. It's suitable for people of all **(1)** _____ , so it might be a good idea for when you bring your students here in June.

They've got a lot of costumes and props and so on which are permanently on **(2)** _____ . It's like a record of the history of the theatre from the fifteenth century to the **(3)** _____ day.

They regularly **(4)** _____ on performances of some of the best known plays. When you're here in June you could all sit **(5)** _____ and watch one of Shakespeare's plays – as **(6)** _____ the weather's alright, that is.

There's also a programme of special activities for groups, **(7)** _____ as workshops and demonstrations. Your students would have **(8)** _____ to go behind the scenes, **(9)** _____ up and even walk on stage.

The good news is you don't have **(10)** _____ to get in. It's open from ten till eight on **(11)** _____ and ten till six on Saturdays. You'd have to book for the special activities **(12)** _____ three weeks in advance, but I could sort that out for you. Anyway, have a **(13)** _____ the website and see what you think.

All the best for now   Elaine

CAE Part 6

Gapped text

For questions **1–6**, read through the text and then choose from the list **(A–I)** the best phrase given below it to fill each of the spaces. Each correct phrase may only be used once. Some of the suggested phrases do not fit at all.

Grown-up gappers

A new trend is creeping upon the massed ranks of the "New Aged": gap years for grown-ups. Once the gap year was a precious time of mind-expanding travel between school and university, and virtually the sole preserve of the eager 18-year-old. **(1)** _____ and heading, usually solo, into the great unknown is being hijacked by increasing numbers of over-50s. As one grown-up gapper puts it, "**(2)** _____ end up saying, 'I could have', instead of 'I did'."

It's an attitude that touches people at all stages of their lives. **(3)** _____ : retirement, bereavement, or the end of a marriage. Others are still in the world of work. Joshua White, who has written a book on the subject, *Taking a Career Break*, says: "When home routines begin to pall and you find yourself craving an opportunity to expose yourself to risk, it is time to give some thought to bringing about a change. Taking a break isn't about self-indulgence, but about having a period in which to regain your balance."

(4) _____ comparable to learning to swim: that moment in childhood of heading out of your depth in the water to discover that instead of sinking, you float. **(5)** _____ , those who put on a pair of jeans and squeeze a *Lonely Planet* guidebook into a back pocket tend to end up refreshed of mind, with a new perspective on life and rediscovered drive and enthusiasm.

Tom Griffiths, founder of *The Gap Year Magazine*, says that over the past few years his website, gapyear.com, has seen an increasing number of hits from the baby-boomer generation. "We call them SKI-ers, which stands for 'spending their kids' inheritance'. **(6)** _____ , but they are every bit as adventurous as youngsters.

A It seems that not all gappers do

B It's for people who don't want to

C More ambitiously, it can be a rite of passage

D These people might be in their fifties and sixties

E Consequently, it marks an end point in one's life

F Now the old idea of leaving one's life behind

G Whatever the motivation might be

H The gap year is now less of a learning experience

I Some discover it at the natural pauses

Writing

CAE Part 2

Leaflets

1 Read the following extract from a leaflet, which was written for students in their final year at college. Write each of these section headings in an appropriate gap **a–c**.

The day of the interview   Practice makes perfect   Do your homework

How to prepare for job interviews

You've been invited for interview and now you want to make sure you do everything within your power to get the job. So what do you need to do to prepare yourself for the big day?

a) _____

(0) *Firstly, you should* find out as much as you possibly can about the position, the company, the industry and even the interviewer. **(1)** *You should go to* your prospective employer's website on the Internet, where the company presents itself as it wants to be seen; relevant trade journals will then tell you how it is viewed by others. **(2)** *You should perhaps also* speak to people who work or have worked for the company, if at all possible.

All this information will give you a great deal to talk about during the interview and so help create the right impression. The more you know, the greater your competitive edge over other candidates.

b) _____

To help increase confidence, many people practise the interview in front of a mirror. However, **(3)** *you should instead* try it out with a real person: it's far more realistic and it gives you the chance to ask him or her for some feedback on your performance.

(4) *In particular, you should practise* answers to common questions you can expect to be asked. These include:

• What do you consider to be your major strengths and weaknesses?
• Why do you want to work for this company?
• Where do you see yourself in five years' time?

An interview is also your chance to decide whether you want to work for the company, so be prepared to ask three or four relevant questions yourself.

c) _____

(5) *You shouldn't ever* underestimate the effect of your appearance on the interviewer: make sure you wear a suit to the interview, even if the normal working environment of the company allows for more informal dress. Punctuality is another crucial factor with regards to first impressions, and for this reason **(6)** *you should always* arrive at the interview site at least 15 minutes before your scheduled meeting.

All that's left now is the interview itself!
See over for information and advice on successful interview strategies.

2 Most of the advice in the leaflet above is introduced with *you should* or *you shouldn't*. It is important in your own writing to include a range of language. Replace each of the numbered phrases **1–6** in the leaflet with one of the expressions in the box. Write each expression in the appropriate space below. There is an example at the beginning **(0)**.

it's always wise to	it would be a mistake to	make a special point of rehearsing
~~the first step is to~~	it's far more advisable to	it's also worthwhile to
the best place to look is		

0 _____ *The first step is to* _____
1 _____   4 _____
2 _____   5 _____
3 _____   6 _____

3 Read the following Writing Part 2 task and do the activities in **A** and **B** below.

Some members of your English class recently commented that they would like to have had more advice at the beginning of the course on how to prepare for the CAE examination. You have agreed to write a leaflet giving a number of ideas and practical tips for future students to read at the start of their CAE exam preparation course.

Write the **text for the leaflet** in approximately 250 words.

A Gathering ideas

i The comments in **1–5** below were all made by students preparing to take the CAE examination. For each one decide which of the following aspects of English the student is focusing on. Each student may be focusing on more than one aspect.

Reading	Listening	Writing
Speaking	Vocabulary	Grammar

1 _____

"Before my lesson on Friday each week, I always spend about an hour in the library doing a Paper 4 test from a past paper – with the headphones on, of course!"

2 _____

"I have two notebooks, one of which I use exclusively for recording new language and structures. In order for it to be a useful reference, I make sure I update and organize it on a regular basis."

3 _____

"I've been visiting the website of an English language newspaper every week, looking at articles which interest me and noting down collocations which I think I might be able to use myself."

4 _____

"It's the Part 1 compulsory question I find the most difficult, especially reports. I'm very busy at work, but I do try and make time to do all the homework my teacher sets for this particular paper – with my effort and her corrections I feel I'm really making progress."

5 _____

"I get together with one of my classmates each week and we spend about an hour comparing and contrasting magazine photos or discussing a range of issues from money to marriage to mobile phones."

ii If possible, add one further idea for each of the different aspects of English mentioned in exercise 1. Would you add any advice which does not fall into these categories?

B Organizing ideas

As in the example on page 90, you might choose to divide your leaflet into three main sections. Which of the following groups of section headings **a–c** would be inappropriate when answering the task above?

a
1 Receptive skills
2 Productive skills
3 Examination skills

b
1 Revising what you have studied
2 Making the most of your time during the exam
3 Life after the CAE exam

c
1 Using the coursebook
2 Preparing with other students
3 Preparing by oneself

4 Now write your answer to the task.

How to go about it

- Organize your ideas from A into relevant sections. You may decide to use one of the appropriate groups of headings in B, or else use your own section headings.
- Decide on an appropriate register for your leaflet.
- Write your answer to the task using some of the advice language from exercise 2. Don't forget to include a brief introduction and ending.

Reading

Gapped text

1 For questions **1–7**, you must choose which of the paragraphs **A–H** on page 93 fit into the gaps in the following magazine article about an attempt to film hippos. There is one extra paragraph which does not fit in any of the gaps.

Hippo Heaven

What happens to a hippo when it sinks beneath the surface? Mzima was the place to find out.

If there's a 'must-see' for a freshwater naturalist in East Africa, then it's *Mzima Spring* in Kenya's *Tsavo West National Park*. I first became aware of it as a teenager, when I was enthralled by Alan and Joan Root's classic film *Mzima: Portrait of a Spring*, with its extraordinary, underwater images of moon-walking hippos. Back then I would have assumed that there were other sites like it, scattered throughout the continent.

1 _____

It was fortunate, then, when my partner Vicky and I eventually got the chance to visit Mzima itself with Alan Root. It was the dry season, and as Alan flew us over Tsavo, the red dust devils spiralled high into the sky. I was looking forward to seeing Mzima for the first time. But when Alan dipped a wing, I was totally unprepared for what leapt out of the monochrome scorched plains and grey lava blocks.

2 _____

I knew immediately that we had to make a film there. At the outset, we had no idea what we could film that would be different from what had been done before. But we believed that if we lived at Mzima for long enough then something would reveal itself. Our goal was to film the behaviour of hippos under water to get some key sequences about which a story could be told. This meant either diving with them so frequently that we gained their trust and they stopped reacting to our presence, or filming them unobserved from an underwater hide.

3 _____

So, after two weeks, we had only spent a total of thirty minutes under water with no film and one attack to show for it. The chance of spending the thousands of hours under water that we would

normally do when making a film looked slim. Hippos are potentially more dangerous than crocodiles, but, the more we explored the spring, the bigger and more numerous the crocodiles we found – and the bolder and more curious they became.

4 _____

At the same time as trying to film under water, we erected towers to give us an aerial view of the spring. From these, we could watch an entire group of hippos and look down through the water. What we saw was exciting. Female hippos were suckling their young under water and defending them against crocodiles. But most extraordinary of all, we could see the hippos opening their mouths under water and having their teeth cleaned by *Labeo* fish, which swarmed inside their gaping jaws.

5 _____

The first time I tried it, this latest hide was secreted in the shallows, in the shade of an overhanging fig tree. I was in there waiting for the hippos to come close, when a troop of baboons arrived to investigate and discovered that the tree was in fruit. As they fed, figs started to rain down from above.

6 _____

At first it wasn't too bad but then the baboons realized that the best figs were in the branches directly above me. All this eating made them thirsty so they descended for a drink before carrying on with the feast. By the time Vicky came to relieve me, this had been going for several hours and the hippos had fled. There was only one thing for it; we would have to set about filming remotely. We ended up with a camera in a housing set on a pan-and-tilt head and fixed to the bed of the spring.

7

It was a revelation to us – the first of many in two years of filming – and just one answer to the question: what happens to a hippo when its nostrils pinch together and it sinks beneath the surface? It also reaffirmed that there is still so much to discover, even about large, charismatic mammals. New knowledge might not come quickly, but it often presents itself if you simply sit and watch.

A I knew only too well what was coming next, but I couldn't escape. The golden rule about hide work is always to have someone else with you when you get in and out; any disturbance is then associated with that person and not the hide. But on this occasion, I was alone.

B It rapidly became apparent that neither method was going to work. When we tried to get into the water with the hippos, they either charged or fled. Meanwhile the local crocodiles became curious, and on the third dive on my way to the hide, I had been forced to fend one off by vigorously hitting it on the head with the camera.

C We were determined to film this under water but progress was dismal. In an idea borrowed from Alan Root, our assistant Norbert Rottcher constructed a new sort of hide, a type of 'reverse aquarium', comprising a large metal 'coffin', open on top, with a glass front through which we could film and stay dry.

D This meant that we couldn't follow the hippos – they had to come to us. In fact, it took nine frustrating months until the hippos gradually got used to it. It was then we discovered that various species of fish were partitioning a hippo's body between them. *Barbels* used their snouts to get between the toes, *Cichlids* cleaned the bristles and tiny *Garra* got in close enough to clean wounds.

E Nestled beneath us was an oasis of liquid turquoise, set in a ring of yellow fever trees. We circled, and each time we passed over, we could see the ruddy forms of hippos asleep in the pool. Through the crystal clear water, we could make out the green shapes of crocodiles and pale blue fish.

F This may be because hippos can't see particularly well under water. They compensate for this by being sensitive to sound, including the high-pitched sound produced by the camera. Despite our efforts, we couldn't muffle it.

G With this in mind, we decided to build a tunnel of protective steel mesh to access the hide more safely. As a solution it seemed obvious, but the hippos evidently found it obvious, too, and they moved away. We then left the hide alone for several months, hoping that the hippos would get used to it, but for some reason, they never did.

H However, when I was filming hippos elsewhere in East Africa for a documentary twenty years later, I discovered that this was not the case. The hippos were swimming in muddy water holes and coffee-coloured rivers, so no matter how exciting the behaviour visible above the surface, every time a hippo's nostrils pinched together, I knew my subject was about to disappear from view.

2 The following words are all used to describe *water* in the text:

a **fresh**water naturalist   **crystal clear** water   **muddy** water holes

Complete each of the gaps below with an appropriate word from the box. The words are all collocates of *water*.

flood	rain	salt	tap	drinking	running	sparkling

1 A "We'd like to drink water with our meal, please."

   B "Certainly, Madam. **Bottled** or _____ **water**?

   A "Bottled, please."

   B "And would you prefer **still** or _____ **water**?

2 Don't fill your bottles up from that tap – it's not safe _____ **water**.

3 We collect _____ **water** in a large tank on the roof, then use it for things like watering the garden or cleaning the car.

4 The merganser is a species of duck which can be seen on either **fresh** or _____ **water**, depending on the time of year.

5 He lives in a house with no electricity, no gas and no _____ **water**.

6 The basement was filled with _____ **water** after a night of torrential rain.

Self help

Add the collocates of **water** to your vocabulary notebook.

Vocabulary

Wordlist on page 215 of the Coursebook.

Verb and noun collocations

1 One of the items of vocabulary in each group is not normally used with the verb in bold. Cross out the item which does not fit. There is an example at the beginning (0).

0 **meet**	a deadline	with success	~~an ambition~~	expectations
1 **deny**	access	on friends	rumours	a criminal charge
2 **lead**	a race	to problems	a life	the truth
3 **welcome**	a decision	someone a favour	an opportunity	comments
4 **keep**	a promise	one's temper	a secret	an effort
5 **pay**	a lie	attention	a compliment	a bill
6 **wish someone**	luck	harm	birth	every happiness

2 Complete the gaps with a verb and noun collocation from exercise 1. Write the appropriate form of the verb. There is an example at the beginning (0).

0 Tom certainly _kept_ his _promise_ to take care of my bicycle; in fact, it's in better condition now than when I lent it to him.

1 Stop talking and _____ _____ !

2 The leader singer has _____ all _____ that the band is splitting up.

3 Environmentalists have _____ the Government's _____ to abandon its controversial nuclear power programme.

4 We _____ you no _____ : we come in peace.

5 I eat the right food, I do regular exercise, I don't smoke; all in all I think I _____ a reasonably healthy _____ .

6 They were disappointed with the restaurant: the food was reasonable, but the service failed to _____ their _____ .

7 It was wrong to shout at him like that; you should have _____ your _____ and told him calmly that his behaviour was unacceptable.

8 He failed to _____ the 10 o'clock _____ set by the newspaper, and his article was not published.

9 The Science Minister explained that journalists had been _____ _____ to the new government laboratories 'in the interests of national security'.

10 I've got my maths exam tomorrow – _____ me _____ !

Approximation

Underline the correct alternative.

1 She probably earns *something/round/upwards* in the region of £80,000 a year.

2 He should be out of hospital in a week or *approximately/about/so*.

3 *Extremely/Very/Quite* nearly 85% of those surveyed said they were in favour of the proposal.

4 *Just/Some/Few* under 3% said they were undecided.

5 I reckon we'll get there *so/something/round* about 6 o'clock, don't you?

6 It's a very exclusive area, with houses costing *upwards/more/over* of £750,000.

7 They estimate there were *many/some/plenty* two and a half million people at the demonstration; that's over half the population of the entire city.

8 The company produces *just/such/something* like 2,000 tons of the stuff every day.

Language focus

 Grammar reference on page 224 of the Coursebook.

Conjunctions

Rewrite each of the sentences using the word given. There is an example at the beginning **(0)**.

0 She wore dark glasses because she didn't want to be recognized. (**so that**)
She wore dark glasses so that she wouldn't be recognized.

1 I don't like boxing, but I still enjoyed the film 'Ali'. (**even**)

_____

2 Two of their players were sent off, but they still won the game. (**despite**)

_____

3 If we don't phone her, she'll worry about us. (**otherwise**)

_____

4 It doesn't matter how I comb it, my hair always looks a mess! (**however**)

_____

5 You might want some more later, so I'll leave the plate there. (**in case**)

_____

6 We spoke very quietly because we didn't want to wake my dad up. (**so as**)

_____

Modal verbs

For questions **1–8** below, use the information in **a** to complete the gap in **b**, which is more formal. Choose from the words in the box. There is an example at the beginning **(0)**.

obliged	obligatory	~~obligation~~	permitted	forbidden
recommended	supposed	required	presumed	

0 a We don't have to give the money back.

  b We are under no *obligation* to refund the money.

1 a You mustn't smoke anywhere in the building.

  b Smoking is not _____ in any part of the building.

2 a They've been told they mustn't speak to the press.

  b They have been _____ to speak to the press.

3 a You really should wear strong shoes.

  b Sturdy footwear is strongly _____ .

4 a You needn't pay until the course finishes.

  b Payment is not _____ until the end of the course.

5 a Don't feel you have to give anything.

  b You should not feel _____ to contribute.

6 a It should have got here a couple of weeks ago.

  b It was _____ to arrive a fortnight ago.

7 a They think he must have left the country.

  b He is _____ to have left the country.

8 a You must wear a seat belt.

  b The wearing of seat belts is _____ .

English in Use

CAE Part 4

Word formation

For questions **1–15**, use the words in the boxes to the right of the texts to form **one** word that fits the same numbered space in the text. The exercise begins with an example **(0)**.

Rainforest Concern

The world's rainforests represent a vast reservoir of **(0)** *knowledge* and hold potential for the **(1)** _____ of new medicines and foods. There is no doubt that large-scale deforestation alters the climate – intensifying droughts in the dry season and floods in the rainy season. The result is fewer animal and plant species, soil **(2)** _____ , a water supply which is **(3)** _____ and poorer health for the local people.

By joining Rainforest Concern and sponsoring acres of **(4)** _____ rainforest for the Choco-Andean Rainforest Corridor in Ecuador, you will be protecting one of the world's most important **(5)** _____ areas. Within these forests live an amazingly high number of seriously **(6)** _____ species of animals, birds and plants. You will also be helping to secure the **(7)** _____ and culture of the Awa and Cayapas indigenous people, who still live in harmony with their natural environment.

For more details on this and other projects, visit our website www.rainforestconcern.org

0	KNOW
1	DISCOVER
2	ERODE
3	RELY
4	THREAT
5	ECOLOGY
6	DANGER
7	SURVIVE

The African white rhino

Together with the Indian rhino, the white rhino is the second **(8)** _____ land mammal in the world: only the elephant beats it for size. Its two distinctive horns, which can measure up to 1.5 metres in **(9)** _____ , are actually **(10)** _____ packed fibres rather than real horns. Its name probably comes from a mistranslation of the Afrikaans word 'weit', **(11)** _____ its wide mouth and not its colour; its thick skin is actually grey. Young white rhinos are quite hairy, in contrast to adults, which are almost **(12)** _____ . The main threat to its **(13)** _____ comes from man, who poaches this and other species of rhino in the **(14)** _____ belief that their horns possess aphrodisiac qualities. Fortunately however, numbers are **(15)** _____ increasing and there are currently over 11,000 white rhinos surviving in the wild.

8	LARGE
9	LONG
10	DENSE
11	DESCRIBE
12	HAIR
13	EXIST
14	MISTAKE
15	STEADY

CAE Part 6   **Gapped text**

For questions **1–6**, read through the text and then choose from the list **(A–I)** the best phrase given below it to fill each of the spaces. Each correct phrase may only be used once. Some of the suggested phrases do not fit at all.

Energy saving in the home

Have you ever stopped to think about how much damage your own home may be doing to the environment? In the UK people's homes are responsible for an alarming 25 per cent of all carbon dioxide emissions. But there are a lot of simple steps that can be taken to put things right and help reduce our CO_2 output.

For a start, get into the habit of clicking off the light switch **(1)** _____ , and swap regular light bulbs for energy-saving versions. These are available in good supermarkets and home stores for around £5 each. And **(2)** _____ to bed, don't just turn off your TV, video/DVD recorder or hi-fi system with the remote control: in standby mode they still use up a lot of energy, so switch them off at the plug socket instead. Washing machines and dishwashers are also hideously wasteful in terms of water, electricity and money **(3)** _____ with less than a full load.

Fridges and freezers should also be used as efficiently as possible. Check the temperature of your fridge: 3°C is ideal and for the freezer it's ¯15°C. Keeping them colder than this is pointless and harmful – it will add between 5 and 10kg of CO_2 emissions for each degree. Never overfill the kettle if all you want is a single mug of tea; don't use large saucepans **(4)** _____ to cook small amounts of food, as they will take longer to heat up. And **(5)** _____ milder in the early spring, you can turn down the central heating by several degrees and run it for fewer hours every day. Summertime air-conditioning in the home may be fashionable, especially for high-spec city apartments, but it's an unnecessary luxury **(6)** _____ to let a breeze blow through is open a window or door.

A when you run them

B when you think it's time

C when it starts to turn

D when it runs out

E when you leave a room

F when all you need to do

G when you only want

H when you have it

I when you go off

CAE Part 3

Error correction

In **most** lines of the following text, there is **either** a spelling **or** a punctuation error. For each numbered line **1–16**, write the correctly spelled word or show the correct punctuation at the end of the line. Some lines are correct. Indicate these lines with a tick (✔). The exercise begins with three examples **(0)**, **(00)** and **(000)**.

The piranha that fell from the sky

0	The Thames is home to over a hundred species of fish but never,	✔
00	until now has a piranha been found in its waters. One of the deadly	_now, has_
000	fish misteriously landed on a boat in Dagenham, having apparently	_mysteriously_
1	fallen out of the sky. The three crew of the Thames Bubbler an	_____
2	environmental vessel which pumps oxygene into the river, identified	_____
3	the razor-toothed fish as a piranha and called in marine experts to	_____
4	investigate Tom Cousins, a fisheries officer at the Environmental	_____
5	Agency, deduced that the fish had been accidentaly dropped by a	_____
6	passing seagull which had plucked it out of the water. Mr Cousins	_____
7	said: "I have to admit, that I was pretty sceptical when I got a call	_____
8	from them telling me that a piranha had fallen out of the sky on to	_____
9	the vessel. But when I saw it, I recognized it by it's shape, and it	_____
10	had a really good pear of teeth on it. It was very fresh and had clearly	_____
11	only just died. You could sea the marks made by the seagull's beak	_____
12	on its back." Mr Cousins though that the fish, normally found in the	_____
13	warmer fresh waters of the Amazon, had probably been realeased by	_____
14	its former owner and swum a long the Thames before it was picked up	_____
15	on wednesday afternoon by a seagull. Piranhas are often kept as pets	_____
16	in Britain, despite the fact they need to be kept in large tanks heated to	_____
	within a very narrow temperature range.	

Writing

CAE Part 2

Proposal

1 Read the following Writing Part 2 task, then complete each of the gaps in the model answer with one of the words or expressions from the box. There is an example at the beginning **(0)**.

The local authority in the town where you are studying has announced its intention to increase the annual budget for environmental projects next year. As a member of a local environmental group you have been asked to submit a proposal for the authorities giving your suggestions. You should give details of how the money should be spent in at least **three** areas, including clear reasons for your recommendations.

Write your **proposal** in approximately 250 words.

therefore	instead	as	in order to
~~the first of these~~	this has led to	also	finally
whilst	clearly	as well as	

Recommendations for environmental projects for the town of Didcup

INTRODUCTION

It is gratifying to observe that the local authority has decided to increase its financial commitment to environmental projects. There are three main areas which require urgent attention and funding.

REDUCING POLLUTION

(0) _The first of these_ is the unacceptably high level of pollution caused by exhaust fumes from cars and lorries, particularly in the town centre. **(1)** _____ a higher incidence of respiratory illness among local inhabitants and a decline in the number of tourists visiting Didcup.

A substantial proportion of the budget should **(2)** _____ be allocated to the creation of more pedestrianized areas within the main shopping district. Money might **(3)** _____ be spent on an awareness raising campaign, encouraging local people to leave their cars at home and use public transport **(4)** _____ .

GREEN AREAS

(5) _____ Didcup boasts a number of parks and gardens, there is a noticeable lack of trees, bushes and flowers on the pavements of our residential areas. **(6)** _____ the obvious aesthetic benefits of these plants to the town, they would release more oxygen into the atmosphere and help further in the fight against pollution. **(7)** _____ , funds would also need to be set aside for the maintenance of these areas throughout the year.

WILDLIFE PROTECTION

(8) _____ , some of the budget should be devoted to the preservation of the town's wildlife. Especially at risk are hedgehogs, hundreds of which are killed each year by traffic. **(9)** _____ protect these much-loved but highly vulnerable animals, traffic signs could be erected in appropriate areas warning drivers to look out for them. This would greatly benefit our gardens **(10)** _____ hedgehogs help control unwanted slugs and snails.

Indeed, all of these measures will make Didcup a much better place for everyone, whether they are resident or tourist, human or animal.

---

2   In the box below write those expressions from the model which refer to spending or using money.

> _increased its financial commitment to_

3   **Either** write your own answer to the task in exercise 1

   or write one of the following proposals.

   1   The principal of your college has been given a budget for the improvement of the learning environment in your college. Write a proposal for your principal, giving details of how the money should be spent in at least **three** areas and including clear reasons for your recommendations.

   2   Your manager at work has been given a budget for the improvement of the working environment in your branch or department. Write a proposal for your manager, giving details of how the money should be spent in at least **three** areas and including clear reasons for your recommendations.

Don't forget!

- Plan your answer carefully.
- As in the model, use a range of vocabulary, structures and linking expressions.
- Write approximately 250 words.

Reading

CAE Part 2

Gapped text

1   For questions **1–6**, choose which of the paragraphs **A–G** on page 101 fit into the gaps in the following magazine article about the history of the baguette, a type of bread from France. There is one extra paragraph which does not fit into any of the gaps.

Give them stick

Steven Kaplan, an American no less, is weaning the French off the travesty of a baguette they have eaten since 1945. John Lichfield reports

You have to be a brave man to mess with a national symbol, especially someone else's national symbol. Steven Kaplan is not just brave, he is heroic. This week, Kaplan, an American, will publish the first gourmet guide to the baguettes of Paris. In Britain, the cliché Frenchman is a grumpy man wearing a beret, gripping a baguette under his arm. In France, the cliché Englishman is a mild man in a bowler with an umbrella over his arm. Like the bowler, the beret has become virtually extinct.

1

Kaplan, a professor of European history, and one of the foremost authorities on the history of bread, calls it something else: 'an impostor, an interloper, a tasteless, aroma-less monstrosity, which has existed for only half a century'. The real French baguette, whose history Kaplan has traced back to the 17th century, began to disappear after the Second World War. Bakers, even small, artisanal bakers, started to adopt modern methods and short-cuts which spawned feather-light, lily-white loaves.

2

By the 1980s, the pre-war baguette, made from double-fermented dough, with no artificial yeast and no chemical additives, had almost gone the way of berets and other French exceptions. It took a campaign by *Real Bread* enthusiasts, including Kaplan, to prod the French government into promoting a retro-baguette revival. In six out of 10 Paris bakeries, far fewer in the provinces, the light, white 'standard baguette' is now sold alongside the succulent, longer-lasting, crunchy baguettes which used to exist in France.

3

After careful consideration of appearance, smell and taste, he has made his choice and come up with a scoring system to grade quality using wheat-sheaves instead of stars. He has awarded 'three wheat-sheaves'

to the best dozen; two 'wheat-sheaves' to another 18; and one 'wheatsheaf' to the rest. Parisian bakers await his book with excitement and foreboding for Kaplan is not just an academic expert: he is a connoisseur, a cheer-leader for bread, a man who trained as a baker, a man whose opinions are respected, even feared, throughout the French bread-making world.

4

Kaplan, who has published four previous books on bread-making and the history of bread, judges baguettes in three ways. A good, traditional baguette should look lumpy and individual, not uniform. Inside, there should be a jumble of uneven apertures in the bread, not a standard pattern of holes. "Smelling the bread, I want my nose to be assaulted by a wide variety of aromas. If I don't get a rich array of aromas, I know that this is a mediocre baguette." The taste of a good baguette should be a balance of sweet and sour, he says. It should "both linger and alter in the mouth."

5

As it happens, part of Kaplan's motivation for writing the book is trying to invent a language in which to describe bread. "We have specific descriptions for wine, but not for bread, which is just as, if not a more important, part of our civilisation. I wanted to try to create a vocabulary for bread which would be supple, flexible and not too pompous."

6

Kaplan hopes his book will lay a trail of crumbs to lead Parisians back on to the path of the true taste of French bread. He prefers not to divulge, pre-publication, the names all of the inaugural "three wheatsheaves" winners, but we can be fairly certain that these may eventually become as prized as three *Michelin* stars.

A They are not the only ones. On the left bank of the city, where two of the capital's best, small bakers, Eric Kayser and Dominique Saibron do business, the conclusions are awaited with some anxiety. "They are bitter rivals," Kaplan says. "They absolutely hate each other, but both make superb traditional baguettes."

B It is this baguette, as defined rigorously by law in France since 1993, which is the principal subject of Kaplan's book, *Cherchez le Pain*. Kaplan has eaten his way, in the past eight months, through 637 of Paris's 1,240 small bakeries searching for and testing this traditional bread. Against all expectations, he remains a very trim man.

C Celebrating, and encouraging, the revival of the old-style baguette, which is still a rarity in some parts of France, is the other thing that drives him. In the general run of Parisian bakeries, the traditional baguette now represents 18 per cent of the turnover in baguettes. In other words, the fluffy, tasteless, white baguette, and its bigger sister, the 'pain', still rule the French table.

D But in fact Kaplan doesn't stop here. Married to a French woman, Kaplan speaks fluent French and often resorts to French words even to describe the texture of bread. His final pronouncement is that the bread beyond the crust should be '*moelleux*'. The wonderfully evocative word has no easy English translation; it means, roughly speaking, moist, soft and velvety.

E The baguette, however, thrives. Or does it? Anywhere in France, and in any pseudo-French baker in the world, you can buy long tubes of fluffy, ultra-white dough, which will set into solid blocks within half a day. The world, including France, refers to this as a baguette or typical 'French loaf'.

F It is impossible to predict how they will react to his conclusions. "The bad news is that half of small bakeries in Paris are producing traditional baguettes which are, quite frankly, awful," says Kaplan. "The good news is that even these bad, traditional baguettes are a hundred times better than standard, white baguettes."

G The French were more than delighted with this. After the dark, lumpy, indigestible bread they'd been forced to endure, the whiter-than-white loaf was very much welcome. It was a fresh start, so to speak, a symbol of modernity.

2 Use the word given in capitals at the end of each line to form a noun that fits in the space in the same line. All the nouns you require appeared in the reading text. There is an example at the beginning **(0)**.

0 She could not hide her *excitement* at the prospect of working with the Australian superstar. **EXCITE**

1 The traditional baguette is currently enjoying a _____ in France. **REVIVE**

2 The book is beautifully illustrated and contains detailed _____ of the most common of our garden birds. **DESCRIBE**

3 Sadly, women in managerial positions are still something of a _____ in my country. **RARE**

4 The government has yet to make an official _____ on the issue. **PRONOUNCE**

5 Against all _____ , she reached the final of the competition. **EXPECT**

6 The company has an annual _____ of £25 million. **TURN**

7 The steam engine was lovingly restored by a group of railway _____ . **ENTHUSIASM**

8 He awaited the results of the medical examination with a certain amount of _____ . **ANXIOUS**

Vocabulary

Wordlist on page 215 of the Coursebook.

Phrasal verbs and prepositions

In **A** and **B** below, complete each of the gaps with one of the prepositions from the relevant box. There is an example at the beginning **(0)**.

A Eating and drinking

at	off	down	up	~~up~~

0 She heated _up_ some of the previous day's stew in the microwave.

1 I polished _____ the remains of that chocolate cake when I got home last night – I was so hungry!

2 When he noticed the time, he gulped _____ the rest of his tea and hurried out.

3 She sat at the table looking sad and dejected, just picking _____ her food.

4 I often go for a run in the morning to work _____ an appetite for breakfast.

B Deception

at	for	into	on

1 He was tricked _____ signing the document, which effectively handed over possession of his house to his nephew.

2 Let's play a trick _____ Stuart – we'll hide all his shoes in the washing machine!

3 My brother confessed to me that he used to cheat _____ cards when we were younger.

4 They've promised us a salary increase if we agree to work overtime, but we're not falling _____ their tricks any more – we know what they're up to.

Expressions with *eat*

1 Complete each of the expressions in bold by writing an appropriate noun in each gap.

bird	hand	home	horse	profits	words

1 When my son and his family come to stay they usually **eat us out of house and _____** : it costs us a small fortune!

2 Judy, our accountant, **has got** the boss **eating out of her _____** : she can get him to do anything she wants.

3 The increase in shoplifting from the company's city centre stores has **eaten into its _____** quite considerably.

4 I always said he'd be a failure, but I was **made to eat my _____** recently when I read he'd become a millionaire three times over.

5 Is dinner nearly ready? I **could eat a _____** !

6 I don't know how that child puts on weight – she **eats like a _____** .

2 Match each of the expressions in **1–6** of exercise 1 with an appropriate meaning **a–e**.

Example: 1 c

a make someone like you so much they do whatever you want
b be forced to admit you were wrong about something
c eat a lot of someone's food when you are a guest in their home
d eat very little
e be extremely hungry
f use up or reduce a part of something, especially time or money

Intensifiers

Match each sentence beginning **1–8** with an appropriate ending **a–h**.

1 All the flights to Manchester were **fully**

2 His new film is a convincing and **deeply**

3 The weather suddenly turned **bitterly**

4 My teenage son is a proud and **fiercely**

5 Prof. Amalric has written several **highly**

6 He's slowly recovering and **desperately**

7 Her next opponent is the **comparatively**

8 The long, hot walk left us feeling **utterly**

a **keen** to get back to work.

b **booked**, so we flew to Heathrow instead.

c **exhausted**, and we all went straight to bed.

d **influential** scientific papers on the subject.

e **moving** tale of one man's battle with alcoholism.

f **cold**, thanks to a chill wind coming from the east.

g **unknown** Pat Dale, who has yet to win a championship.

h **independent** child, but he still likes a cuddle from his mum.

Self help

Study the adverb + adjective collocations in bold in the exercise above for one minute. Then cover the sentence endings a–f and look only at the beginnings 1–6. How many collocations can you remember?

Language focus

 Grammar reference on page 225 of the Coursebook.

Comparisons

In each of the following sentences one of the words is incorrect. Find the word and change it. There is an example at the beginning **(0)**.

0 The food wasn't quite as spicy as I'd been told it might be and overall I enjoyed the meal, as ~~had~~ everyone else in my family.
    did

1 By far the dullest job I've ever had was when I worked like a security guard in a high street clothes shop in Macclesfield.

2 It wasn't so much Ralph's good looks which appealed to Eleanor and attracted her to him than his warm effervescent personality.

3 Everyone said the listening exam was much more difficult than they thought it would be, but I didn't think it was anywhere close as hard as the ones we'd done in class.

4 I much prefer our local supermarket to any of those huge out-of-town hypermarkets: apart from being a great amount more convenient, it's quite a lot cheaper, too.

5 I can't understand why the film was such hugely successful: it wasn't nearly as good as his last one, yet it made five times as much at the box office.

6 The more freedom you give children and the fewer limits you impose on them, the more unruly they become, in much the same way that certain types of plant, which will overrun a garden if they are not regularly cut back and held in check.

English in Use

CAE Part 1

Multiple-choice cloze

For questions **1–15**, read the text below and then decide which answer **A, B, C** or **D** best fits each space. The exercise begins with an example **(0)**.

The ready meal capital of Europe

In recent years, ready-made meals have **(0)** ___ Britain's eating **(1)** ___ . Britons now spend four times as **(2)** ___ as the Italians on ready-made meals and six times more than the Spanish. Demand for **(3)** ___ meals has increased across Europe as a **(4)** ___ , but why has Britain become the **(5)** ___ European capital of ready-made food, second only in the world to America?

Convenience is **(6)** ___ of the attraction. A recent survey **(7)** ___ that 77 per cent of purchasers said they only bought ready meals when they did not have time to cook. Dr Susan Jebb, head of nutrition at the Medical Research Council, said: "People in the UK work the **(8)** ___ hours, we are very time-poor, and we don't have a strong cultural history of cooking."

The ready-made meal **(9)** ___ also reflects changing social **(10)** ___ in Britain. More people live alone and so are less likely to be **(11)** ___ to cook. And with families eating together less often, ready-meals allow people to eat what they want when they want. Julia Michna, of Marks and Spencer, says that ready meals also reflect changing **(12)** ___ in food. "Britain's multiculturalism has brought a **(13)** ___ range of restaurants than other European countries, and ethnic cuisines, which people are often scared of cooking from scratch, are **(14)** ___ more popular. One quarter of chilled meals are Indian, and nearly one in five is Chinese."
Ms Michna said that traditional British food **(15)** ___ only 18 per cent of sales.

0	**A** amended	**B** adjusted	**C** transferred	**D** <u>transformed</u>
1	**A** ways	**B** forms	**C** habits	**D** terms
2	**A** equal	**B** same	**C** much	**D** more
3	**A** immediate	**B** instant	**C** urgent	**D** direct
4	**A** conclusion	**B** total	**C** sum	**D** whole
5	**A** unclaimed	**B** unclassified	**C** undefeated	**D** undisputed
6	**A** element	**B** piece	**C** part	**D** share
7	**A** found	**B** made	**C** put	**D** gave
8	**A** hardest	**B** longest	**C** widest	**D** largest
9	**A** bang	**B** bash	**C** bump	**D** boom
10	**A** trends	**B** flows	**C** drifts	**D** movements
11	**A** convinced	**B** bothered	**C** worried	**D** disturbed
12	**A** desires	**B** likings	**C** tastes	**D** wishes
13	**A** longer	**B** deeper	**C** harder	**D** wider
14	**A** very	**B** quite	**C** far	**D** such
15	**A** comprised of	**B** accounted for	**C** responded to	**D** participated in

CAE Part 4   **Word formation**

For questions **1–15**, use the words in the boxes to the right of the texts to form **one** word that fits the same numbered space in the text. The exercise begins with an example **(0)**.

Don't forget!

- Look at the words before and after each space to help you choose the correct part of speech.
- You may need to use the negative or plural form of a noun.
- You may need to use the negative form of an adjective or adverb.

A Vegetarian Cookbook

If you often have **(0)** _difficulty_ knowing what to serve for a mixed **(1)** _____ of vegetarians and non-vegetarians, _Vegetarian Dishes for All_ is a definite must-have. Its **(2)** _____ range of mouth-watering soups, starters, salads, pasta dishes, gratins and desserts provides ample **(3)** _____ to the most sceptical of meat-eaters that vegetarian food is not automatically dull in flavour or **(4)** _____ in appearance. The recipes, which are **(5)** _____ straightforward, will teach both the novice and the expert how to cook vegetables creatively and with spectacular results. Easy-to-find ingredients are used in a wide range of inspiring **(6)** _____ , which will delight every one of your guests, and elevate your cooking skills to new **(7)** _____ .

0	DIFFICULT
1	GATHER
2	IMAGINE
3	PROVE
4	ATTRACT
5	REFRESH
6	COMBINE
7	HIGH

Oily Fish

Fatty fish like salmon, mackerel and sardines are known to have **(8)** _____ properties. Oily fish all contain omega-3 fatty acids. These help to **(9)** _____ levels of blood fats called triglycerides and reduce blood clotting, both of which are important in **(10)** _____ protection against heart disease. Omega-3 oils also help to reduce **(11)** _____ , which means they could alleviate symptoms of rheumatoid arthritis like morning joint **(12)** _____ and pain, as well as improving joint **(13)** _____ . Other positive benefits include a **(14)** _____ risk of having a stroke, and there's evidence that oily fish may protect against an age-related eye disease: Australian **(15)** _____ found that people who ate fatty fish more than once a week were half as likely to develop macular degeneration as those who ate fish less than once a month.

8	MEDICINE
9	LOW
10	PROVIDE
11	INFLAME
12	STIFF
13	MOBILE
14	REDUCE
15	RESEARCH

CAE Part 2

Open cloze

For questions **1–15**, complete the following article by writing **one** word in each space. The exercise begins with an example **(0)**.

> ## Distraction burglaries
>
> **(0)** _An_ estimated 3,000 highly mobile criminals are earning **(1)** _____ to £40 million a year by robbing and tricking elderly people **(2)** _____ of cash, in many cases their life savings. Some 300,000 pensioners are falling victim **(3)** _____ "distraction burglaries" each year, say police. Three quarters of victims are women, **(4)** _____ an average age of 81. Nine out of 10 victims live alone.
>
> Many victims feel **(5)** _____ have been complicit in some ways by letting the thieves trick their way **(6)** _____ their homes and keep quiet about losing money or property, believing relatives may prevent **(7)** _____ living on their own. Crimes range from simple distraction of the victim by one thief – possibly posing **(8)** _____ a policeman or gas or electricity worker, **(9)** _____ others burgle a house – to the extortion of large amounts of money for poor quality work on houses or gardens.
>
> The scale of distraction burglaries **(10)** _____ only emerged recently. Around 16,000 such offences are recorded in England and Wales each year. Thieves will travel hundreds **(11)** _____ miles in a day to find victims and to avoid police. They often operate as families, using children **(12)** _____ young as six to distract victims, for example by kicking a ball into their garden. Profits **(13)** _____ thought to be considerable: one family of thieves was found **(14)** _____ have £3.5 million in assets, with **(15)** _____ sign of legitimate employment whatsoever.

Writing

CAE Part 1

Formal letter and article

Read the following Writing Part 1 task.

You are the Secretary of the English Club at the school where you are studying in Britain. The club recently organized a successful evening at a local restaurant and the Director of Studies would like you to write an article about it for the school magazine.

You have also decided to write to the manager of the restaurant thanking him and his staff for their contribution to the evening's success and suggesting improvements for future club dinners.

Read the note from the Director of Studies together with the advertisement and the letter from the restaurant manager on which you have made some notes. Then, **using the information appropriately,** write:

a an **article** for the school magazine (approximately 150 words);

b an appropriate **letter** to the owner of the restaurant (approximately 100 words).
  You do not need to include postal addresses.

You should use your own words as far as possible.

> *The dinner was certainly a success, wasn't it? Everyone enjoyed themselves and it was marvellous to see students speaking in English with each other about so many different topics. Shame about the seating arrangements, but I was pleased to see that once things got going, everyone started swapping places in order to talk to different people.*
>
> *I'd be really grateful if you could write an article for the school magazine about the evening. I'd like the dinner to become a regular event, and an article would be a great way to advertise it and encourage others to come along. 25 students – and 5 teachers – was a very good turnout considering it was the first time, but the more we can get the better. Let's see if we can fill out the whole restaurant next time!*
>
> *Thanks*

The English Club
invites you to its first
Club Dinner
7.30pm on Tuesday, November 11th
at the Cosmopolitan Restaurant

Speak English with <u>teachers and other students</u> as you enjoy a
<u>3-course meal</u> in relaxed surroundings. <u>No matter what your level</u>,
it'll be a great way to meet others and practice your English!
Book your place now at reception.
Price: £25

*brilliant food –
for example …*

*and the waiters and
waitresses – really
nice to everyone*

*several beginners
and low intermediate
students there*

Dear Sir/Madam

I am writing to confirm your booking at the
Cosmopolitan Restaurant for 30 diners on Tuesday
11th November.

We have devised <u>a menu</u> which we hope will be to
everyone's taste and which includes a choice of 3
starters, 3 main courses and 3 desserts. The total cost
will be £900, or £25 per head: this price does not
include <u>drinks</u>. The restaurant will be open to other
diners, but we will ensure that all members of your
party are <u>seated together</u>.

We look forward to seeing you on the 11th.

Yours faithfully

Richard Ashley

Manager

*no vegetarian
options*

*wine very
expensive*

*one long table –
not ideal*

How to go about it

- Read the question and all the input material again, underlining key information which will be important for your answer.
- Make two lists, one of those points which will be relevant for your letter, and another of relevant points for your article.
- Write two plans, arranging the points in each list in a logical order.
- Write your answer using an appropriate register for each task.

Don't forget!

- One of the aims of your article is to encourage students to participate in future Club Dinners.
- The aim of your letter is not to complain, but to thank and make suggestions for improvements.

Reading

Multiple matching

For questions **1–22**, answer by choosing from the sections of the article **(A–I)**. Some of the choices may be required more than once.

In which section does the writer mention the following?

a time when she understands most clearly what it means to be homeless	1 ____
the suggestion that people are less likely to give money to people who look genuinely poor	2 ____
a sense of shame about the way in which she received a form of charity	3 ____ 4 ____ 5 ____
her discomfort preventing her from caring about the impression she is making	6 ____
regret over the fact that she had chosen the wrong item	7 ____
her firm conviction that she can depend on the charity of others	8 ____
the inability to make up her mind causing her to miss an opportunity	9 ____
a sense of belonging that she experienced for the first time	10 ____
an occasion when she performed her own act of generosity	11 ____ 12 ____
the generosity of someone who was less fortunate than her	13 ____
her determination to acquire money through a new approach	14 ____ 15 ____ 16 ____
a feeling of real fear regarding her situation	17 ____
her surprise at receiving what she had asked for	18 ____ 19 ____ 20 ____
her awareness of the importance of repaying what she owes	21 ____
someone else's suspicion regarding her motives	22 ____

Who needs money when you've got a spring in your step?

How hard can it be to live on your wits in London for the day? **Hermione Eyre** *left home one sunny morning without a care in the world – or a penny in her purse ... .*

A I step out of the front door into a bright morning. I've left my cash card, wallet and phone on my bed and emptied my pockets of loose change. All I have is a warm scarf and a springy step. I'm off to try my luck on the streets of London for a day. And on this fine morning, I feel confident entrusting myself to the charity of those living in the city. First objective: breakfast. I trot into my local café, which I visit perhaps every other morning. It's a fashionable little place specialising in marzipan animals. I can't imagine it'll welcome a scrounger like myself. I say 'Hello, I haven't got any money. Can I have a coffee?' The woman smiles indulgently, and sets the bean-grinder whirring. Well, this could be a great day! Of course, it's probably because I'm a familiar face that she has no problem giving me credit.

B This certainly makes me feel part of a supportive local community I never knew existed. The Turkish newsagent round the corner, someone later told me, also offers goods on credit to familiar faces. I am conscious that the system depends on trust however, and honour my debt at the café the next day. Anyway, I've had my caffeine and I'm managing. I don't need public transport, I think, as a bus crammed with workers grinds past. I'm lightstepping into town, heading, like so many indigent people, to Soho. On the way, I fall into step with Leo. He's sleeping in a hostel and wants to become a journalist. I ask him his tips on getting around London for free, but if he has any he is too proud to share them. I try to explain I'm experimenting with going without money. He misunderstands and digs into his coat and tries to give me some coins.

C Guilty and a little humiliated, I say goodbye and head off. The weather's changed and it's starting to spit. I linger in a tobacconist's, touching up the newspapers, but the proprietor starts tutting at me. Looking for another place to shelter I notice the *Conway Hall Ethical Society and Humanist Library*. Sounds just the job. I dart inside. It's warmish and echoing with distant voices. Suddenly, a man strides past, carrying an enormous platter piled high with spring rolls. My body stays still but my eyes follow the platter down the corridor. I want to ask for one but waste fatal moments in embarrassed indecision. Then, figuring that, as a Humanist, he can hardly say no, I skip after him, but too slow. A big door shuts behind him.

D Busking it is then. In Soho, I shelter in a doorway and polish my harmonica. I set my cap down in front of me, find a coin in the gutter and pop it into the cap. Hopefully, money will follow money. I start to blow. It's a truly terrible sound, like a tin bagpipe, but I'm too cold and too hungry to be bothered about it. I blow with ear-twisting soulfulness for an hour. My net gain is approximately 25 pence. Then, to my unexpected delight, my fortunes change. A gentleman in a hat mumbles 'good luck' and drops me £1.20. He disappears before I can see his face or thank him. I play a last triumphal chord, then hobble off.

E With my earnings, I can afford a minestrone soup (£1.30) at a small restaurant. So I go in and order it right away. I should have known better. They serve me the pauper's option within seconds, bill me, then shoo me on to the pavement. The whole thing is over in 10 minutes flat. If I'd had any street sense, I'd have known that, to maximize my time in the warm, I should have pored over the menu, savoured some tap water, enquired grandly after the fish of the day, then plumped for, oh the minestrone, 'for the moment…'.

F Instead, I'm outside wandering the windy Covent Garden piazza. I steal a sugar lump from a bar. I sit in the public toilets trying to get warm. Then I pull myself together again and decide to try to trade on my energy and will to work. I ask a sandwich-board man how he got his job but he growls 'No jobs!' presuming, perhaps, that I wanted his. I offer to wash glasses in a pub, to push a postman's trolley, to help a street vendor. But they all laugh and say no. I like to think this says more about the stringency of health and safety regulations than it does about my employability.

G It's no time to give up. I have to be a bit more enterprising. I sit in a doorway ripping up strips of coloured paper and doodling horoscope predictions on them. Superstition sells, I hope. I do wobbly little pictures, and write things like 'Gemini: wear more red.' I hawk them around Bond Street. Only one sells, for 20p. Then I see, among the tourists, a lady with a packed lunch. I sidle closer. She's got a lovely tangerine. She's wearing a 'One World, One Family' badge. I'm ashamed to admit that 'easy target' came to mind. I ask her for her tangerine, and she gives it freely. As we part, I slip her a smart new eyeshadow from my bag, certainly more costly than the item of fruit, but the least I can do.

H People are extraordinarily kind to me but their generosity seems to dwindle as my need increases. Early on, when I looked like a nice presentable kid, people gave to me easily. The wide community of the middle class looks after its own it appears. But it's much harder to get people's sympathy and donations now that I look bedraggled and slightly desperate. It's early evening when I enter *Pizza Express* and offer to wash dishes in return for garlic bread. The manager, an angel in a suit, pats me on the back. 'Margherita pizza OK for you?'. He says: 'You're young, things are hard in London.' I'm stunned by his kindness, more than I'd dared hope for. He hands me a warm takeaway box which I scamper off with. I approach a real tramp and invite him to share the pizza with me. He soon gets into it. With his second bite he asks loudly 'And to drink?' and bursts into laughter. I laugh too. It's the best pizza I've ever tasted.

I It's getting late now, and the streets are deserted. I feel daunted by the long journey home. One ankle is twisted, the other foot has seized up. It's 10pm by the time I reach Tottenham Court Road and I have a growing sense of panic. I have no money for transport, no way of ringing anyone. For the first time, I feel genuinely terrified. Drunk people laugh at me and I feel vulnerable. I want to call after them 'I'm really one of you!' Eventually, I crawl on the back of a bus and plead with the conductor – something I swore I'd never do, because it puts him in such a difficult position. I feel immoral and degraded. I stumble home about midnight. My feet don't heal for a week. In the final hour, I've gained a deep and genuine insight into what it might really be like to be destitute and living on the streets. Absolutely horrible.

Vocabulary

Wordlist on page 215 of the Coursebook.

Money

Complete each of the gaps with one of the words from the box.

redundancy	counterfeit	sponsorship
pocket	ransom	housekeeping

1 Several members of a criminal gang have been arrested on charges of printing and passing _____ **money**.

2 Some parents give their children far too much _____ **money** each week.

3 She could never afford to buy meat or fish because her husband used to spend half the _____ **money** in the pub on Friday night.

4 The kidnappers released the hostages two hours after the _____ **money** was paid.

5 The factory where he worked was forced to close down and he used some of his _____ **money** to pay off his mortgage.

6 I swam 163 lengths of the pool non-stop and raised over £500 in _____ **money**, which I donated to a local hospital.

Verbs usually associated with money

1 For questions **1–5**, underline the correct verb **A, B, C** or **D**.

1 The discovery of a second set of fingerprints _____ **weight to the theory** that Brooks did not act alone.
   A owes   **B** pays   **C** lends   **D** invests

2 The Minister _____ **tribute to** rescue workers for their 'courage in the face of adversity'.
   A sold   **B** paid   **C** lent   **D** spent

3 I know a quicker way to get there if you want to _____ **some time**.
   A invest   **B** spend   **C** save   **D** borrow

4 The French writer _____ **the idea** for his first novel **from** an old Russian folk tale.
   A borrowed   **B** bought   **C** saved   **D** charged

5 The company _____ **its success** to the quality of its products.
   A pays   **B** lends   **C** sells   **D** owes

2 Which of the correct verbs in exercise 1 collocates with each group of nouns?

1 _____ a compliment/attention/one's respects

2 _____ a favour/an apology/an explanation

3 _____ support/credibility/assistance

4 _____ effort/energy

5 _____ a word/a phrase

Self help

Add the **Verbs usually associated with money** to your vocabulary notebook, together with the nouns which collocate with them.

3 Complete the gaps using appropriate verb and noun collocations from exercise 2. Write the correct form of the verb, and if necessary, use an article (*a/an*) with the noun. There is an example at the beginning **(0)**.

0 I didn't really hear what he said; I wasn't *paying* much *attention*, to be honest.

1 It seems I _____ you _____ ; I doubted your honesty, and clearly I was wrong. I hope you can forgive me.

2 Over a hundred people came to the funeral to _____ their last _____ to the woman who had done so much for the local community.

3 In order to refer to the first night of a film or a play, English has _____ the French _____ 'premiere', meaning 'first'.

4 I had to help him, really – I felt I _____ him _____ for that time he fixed my car for me.

5 When I said your new hairstyle was 'different', it wasn't a criticism: on the contrary, I was _____ you _____ .

Language focus

G Grammar reference on page 225 of the Coursebook.

Noun phrases

1 Complete each of the gaps with one of the words from the box.

chances	depths	height	matter	grain
sense	sign	source	state	pack

1 I keep forgetting people's names; I think it must be **a _____ of age**.

2 It's not exactly **a _____ of life and death**, but I would appreciate it if you could get it done as soon as possible.

3 There wasn't **a _____ of truth** in what he said – his speech was **a _____ of lies** from start to finish.

4 I felt **an enormous _____ of relief** when I heard I'd passed.

5 After the rioting, the government declared **a _____ of emergency**, calling out the troops and imposing a night-time curfew.

6 I have no investments or savings, so the state pension is my only **_____ of income**.

7 Whether you're in **the _____ of winter** or **the _____ of summer**, AirFlow® ensures the temperature inside your home is exactly how you want it.

8 The team's **_____ of promotion** to the First Division suffered a blow yesterday when they lost at home to relegation candidates Bristol City.

2 There is one mistake in each of the following sentences. Find the mistakes and correct them. There is an example at the beginning **(0)**.

     lamb

0 We had ~~lamb's~~ chops for lunch yesterday.

1 I'm going to get another beer can – I'm really thirsty.

2 He tried to turn the handle of door, but realized he'd been locked in.

3 She didn't have an evidence's scrap to support her accusations.

4 She gave me several useful advice pieces on cooking with pastry.

5 We had to write a three pages essay on the importance of money in today's society.

6 The hotel could only guarantee him a week work.

7 They gazed in wonder at the snow-covered mountains' tops.

8 I read about it in last April edition of *Gardening Monthly*.

English in Use

CAE Part 2   **Open cloze**

For questions **1–15**, complete the following article by writing **one** word in each space. The exercise begins with an example **(0)**.

The sales

It is December. The first frost and snow of winter **(0)** _are_ upon us and, as **(1)** ____ drawn by some mysterious force, otherwise sane, ordinary people are getting up at 5am **(2)** ____ queue for hours in the cold and dark. The sales have begun. Before Christmas!

As mere amateur bargain-hunters have always suspected, **(3)** ____ is a black art to sales shopping. Cunning sales veterans, determined to avoid the horrid changing-room queue, do their trying-on weeks **(4)** ____ advance. Then, **(5)** ____ the doors are flung open, they'll push, elbow and lock coat-hangers with **(6)** ____ another to reach the object **(7)** ____ their desire. This Darwinian struggle is carried **(8)** ____ in a terribly polite way, as everybody else pretends that everybody else **(9)** ____ being "so pushy".

Their treasures clutched to their breast, their cheerfulness is barely disguised, in **(10)** ____ of the uncomfortable weight of armfuls of plates, dishes, sheets and towels. The only shadow is the sight of other attractive bargains **(11)** ____ picked out by fellow shoppers.

People rarely do their sales shopping **(12)** ____ their own; it's mostly done in a threesome of mothers and daughters. They argue about skirt lengths and bathrobe colours, but **(13)** ____ shines through is a sense of unshakeable warmth, support and mutual understanding. The same is true **(14)** ____ men: they stand outside, holding bags and bonding in **(15)** ____ own 'What are we doing here?' way. Sales shopping certainly brings people together.

CAE Part 3   **Error correction**

In **most** lines of the following text, there is **either** a spelling **or** a punctuation error. For each numbered line **1–16**, write the correctly spelled word or show the correct punctuation at the end of the line. Some lines are correct. Indicate these lines with a tick (✔). The exercise begins with three examples **(0)**, **(00)** and **(000)**.

Winning the lottery

0	Imagine you've won the lottery. You've been picked up by a limousine,	✔
00	posed with the super-sized cheque and had your fill of champane. What	_champagne_
000	next? Should you quit your job Split the money with your family and	_job?_
1	freinds? Invest it? Give it to charity or head off round the world? These	_____
2	are some of the questions lottery milionaires have to deal with. The	_____
3	answers have set most of them – on the road to happiness – but others on	_____
4	the road to ruin. In America and Britain many winners have started	_____
5	businesses or made there families' lives more comfortable. Others have	_____
6	gone bankrupt, got divorced or even committed suicide. The UK's	_____
7	National Lottery says it urges all of its winners to be cautiuos. Paula	_____
8	McEvoy, a spokeswoman, says: It's a shock to the system, but one with	_____
9	a very big upside. We advise them not to make a quick decission. They	_____
10	should put it in a bank or building society acount and leave it alone until	_____
11	they come to terms with it." It is sound advice Even if interest rates are	_____
12	low, putting the money somewhere safe gives you time, to look at the	_____
13	options on offer from different institutions. It also lets you forget about the	_____
14	serious business of financial planing until you've had the chance to enjoy	_____
15	an impromptu holiday or other treat. The company advises winners too	_____
16	make new wills as soon as possible and seek profesional financial advice.	_____

CAE Part 5   **Register transfer**

For questions **1–13**, read the following informal note and use the information in it to complete the numbered gaps in the advertisement. The words you need **do not occur** in the note. **Use no more than two words in each gap**. The exercise begins with an example **(0)**.

NOTE

Nick

Here's the info I'd like you to use for the ad in the local newspaper:

- we realize that everyone's different so we've got various savings accounts to satisfy different people's requirements;
- mention in particular our 'Premium' fixed-term savings accounts with high interest, and the 'Ready Money' accounts for people who need to get to their money quickly. Customers can switch between accounts with no penalties;
- they can take out up to £500 a day from normal accounts and £3,000 from high-interest accounts, as long as they give us two weeks' notice;
- they can open an account by calling in at their local branch – they have to be at least 18 years old and they have to show something to prove that they are who they say they are;
- remember the special offer that we'll pay £50 into the account of new clients. The offer closes on 18th April so tell them to apply immediately;
- if they've got any questions our branch staff will be happy to help them.

Jill

ADVERTISEMENT

Here at Mundibank we understand that people are not the **(0)** _same as_ each other.

That's why we offer a wide **(1)** _____ savings accounts, designed to **(2)** _____ needs of different types of customers. You might for example choose one or our high-earning fixed-term 'Premium Savings Accounts', or alternatively, if you need instant **(3)** _____ to your funds, a 'Ready Money Account'. And if your circumstances change, you can switch your money from one account **(4)** _____ with no penalties. You can **(5)** _____ as much as £500 each day from our regular accounts and up to £3,000 from 'Premium Accounts', **(6)** _____ that you inform us two weeks in advance.

To open an account, just pay **(7)** _____ to your local branch. The **(8)** _____ age requirement is 18 and you will need to show proof **(9)** _____ . As a special offer to new customers, Mundibank will **(10)** _____ their account with an extra £50. The offer only **(11)** _____ until 18th April, so open your new account without **(12)** _____ . If you have any queries, speak to the staff at your local branch, who will be pleased to offer their **(13)** _____ .

Writing

Read the Paper 2 Writing tasks below. Before you write your answer, read the *How to go about it box* and do the *Key vocabulary* exercises on page 115.

Choose **one** of the following writing tasks. Your answer should follow exactly the instructions given. Write approximately 250 words.

1 Your region has recently been affected by adverse weather conditions, which have caused a great deal of damage to property and agriculture, as well as disrupting services and communications. A friend of yours from abroad has written to you expressing concern after seeing television pictures of some of the damage. Write a **letter** to your friend to reassure him or her, describing what happened, how your region has been affected and what is being done to tackle the situation.

2 You see this announcement in an English language magazine.

> **Competition**
>
> **A place to live in**
>
> We'd like to hear how readers feel about the village, town or city where they are currently living. How satisfied are you and what would you change about it? Write and tell us about at least two changes you would make saying how the place would benefit from these changes and how they would affect you personally.
>
> The best entry will win two free air tickets to the town of their choice!

Write your **entry** for the competition.

3 You are a member of the sports and social club in the town in Britain where you are studying. You have been asked to produce a leaflet in English aimed at encouraging other foreign students to become members.

Your leaflet should:
- inform students about some of the facilities and activities that are available
- outline the benefits of being a member of the club
- encourage students to join.

Write the **text for the leaflet**.

4 There is a feeling amongst employees in your workplace that your department is seriously understaffed. You have been asked to write a report for the Managing Director, giving details of how the situation might be improved.

You should:
- describe the current situation and its effect on the department and its staff
- recommend how many new employees should be taken on and what jobs they should be given
- say how this would improve your department's performance.

Write your **report**.

How to go about it

- Select your Part 2 task carefully. Consider, in particular, whether you will be able to demonstrate a good range of vocabulary and structures when answering the task. The *Key vocabulary* exercises are designed to give you some help with this important aspect of the task.
- You should not attempt the final, work-related task unless you have experience of a relevant work situation.
- Plan your answer carefully before writing it. Follow the checklist of points for planning and checking your work on page 193 of the Coursebook.

Key vocabulary

Task 1

1 Match each of the adjectives **1–5** with an appropriate noun **a–e**.

1 torrential   a flooding
2 gale-force   b storm
3 widespread   c rain
4 a violent   d snow
5 thick   e winds

2 Complete each of the gaps with one of the nouns from the box.

Families
Power lines
Crops
Tiles
Roads

1 _____ were blown off roofs by high winds.
2 _____ were brought down by falling trees.
3 _____ were flooded out of their homes.
4 _____ were blocked by deep snow drifts.
5 _____ were destroyed in farming areas.

Task 2

demolished
pedestrianized
built
installed
introduced

Complete each of the gaps with one of the verbs from the box, then match each sentence beginning **1–5** with an appropriate ending **a–e**.

1 More street lighting should be _____   a to keep the town's youth out of trouble.
2 The shopping district should be _____   b to increase security at night.
3 The disused railway station should be _____   c to improve transport links with the nearest town.
4 A new sports centre should be _____   d to make way for a children's playground.
5 A more frequent bus service should be _____   e to reduce traffic pollution in the town centre.

Task 3

organizes
boasts
provides
keeps
entitles

Complete each of the gaps with one of the verbs from the box.

1 Our centre _____ an Olympic-sized indoor swimming pool.
2 Membership _____ you to make full use of our excellent facilities.
3 The club _____ you with the perfect opportunity to meet new people.
4 The committee _____ a wide range of social events.
5 Regular exercise _____ your body in shape and helps beat stress.

Task 4

morale
strain
effectiveness
duties
deadlines

Complete each of the gaps with one of the nouns from the box.

1 The situation is **putting a great** _____ **on** staff.
2 The department is finding it increasingly difficult to **meet** _____ .
3 New staff should be **allocated** _____ in the following areas.
4 These changes would help **boost** _____ amongst demotivated staff.
5 They would also **improve the** _____ of the company as a whole.

Before you write

For more information and useful language for each of the tasks, consult the relevant pages in the Ready for Writing unit in the Coursebook.

Word formation list

Nouns

-age

Verb	Noun
break	breakage
cover	coverage
pack	package
post	postage
store	storage
wreck	wreckage

Adjective	Noun
short	shortage

-al

Verb	Noun
(dis)approve	(dis)approval
arrive	arrival
bury	burial
deny	denial
dismiss	dismissal
propose	proposal
rehearse	rehearsal
remove	removal
renew	renewal
revive	revival
survive	survival

-ance

Verb	Noun
annoy	annoyance
(dis)appear	(dis)appearance
attend	attendance
disturb	disturbance
endure	endurance
enter	entrance
ignore	ignorance
inherit	inheritance
perform	performance
rely	reliance
resemble	resemblance
resist	resistance
signify	(in)significance
tolerate	(in)tolerance

Adjective	Noun
arrogant	arrogance
distant	distance
(un)important	(un)importance
(ir)relevant	(ir)relevance
reluctant	reluctance

-ence

Verb	Noun
confide	confidence
depend	(in)dependence
differ	difference
exist	existence
insist	insistence
obey	obedience
occur	occurrence
offend	offence
persist	persistence
recur	recurrence

Adjective	Noun
absent	absence
competent	(in)competence
(in)convenient	(in)convenience
evident	evidence
innocent	innocence
intelligent	intelligence
(im)patient	(im)patience
present	presence
violent	violence

-cy

Adjective	Noun
(in)accurate	(in)accuracy
(in)adequate	(in)adequacy
(in)appropriate	(in)appropriacy
(in)decent	(in)decency
(in)efficient	(in)efficiency
(in)frequent	(in)frequency
immediate	immediacy
infant	infancy
intimate	intimacy
(il)literate	(il)literacy
pregnant	pregnancy
private	privacy
redundant	redundancy
secret	secrecy
urgent	urgency
vacant	vacancy

-dom

Adjective	Noun
bored	boredom
free	freedom
wise	wisdom

Person	Abstract noun
king	kingdom
star	stardom

-ful

Noun	Noun (Quantity)
arm	armful
cup	cupful
fist	fistful
hand	handful
house	houseful
room	roomful
spoon	spoonful

-hood

Person	Abstract noun
adult	adulthood
child	childhood
father	fatherhood
man	manhood
mother	motherhood
neighbour	neighbourhood*
parent	parenthood
woman	womanhood

*neighbourhood
part of a town or city where people live

Adjective	Noun
likely	likelihood

-iety

Adjective	Noun
anxious	anxiety
notorious	notoriety
sober	sobriety
various	variety

-ity

Adjective	Noun
(un)able	(in)ability
(in)active	(in)activity
complex	complexity
credible	credibility
curious	curiosity
(un)equal	(in)equality
(un)familiar	(un)familiarity
ferocious	ferocity
(in)flexible	(in)flexibility
(in)formal	(in)formality
generous	generosity
hostile	hostility
immune	immunity
intense	intensity
major	majority
minor	minority
(im)mobile	(im)mobility
objective	objectivity
(un)original	(un)originality
personal	personality
(un)popular	(un)popularity
prosperous	prosperity
(im)pure	(im)purity
(in)secure	(in)security
(in)sensitive	(in)sensitivity
severe	severity
similar	similarity
simple	simplicity
(in)sincere	(in)sincerity
stupid	stupidity
subjective	subjectivity
(in)valid	(in)validity

-ing

Verb	Noun
advertise	advertising
build	building
gather	gathering
like	liking
live	living
meet	meeting
record	recording
say	saying
set	setting
suffer	suffering

Word formation list

-ment

Verb	Noun
achieve	achievement
(dis)agree	(dis)agreement
amaze	amazement
amuse	amusement
announce	announcement
argue	argument
arrange	arrangement
commit	commitment
content	contentment
develop	development
disappoint	disappointment
discourage	discouragement
embarrass	embarrassment
employ	(un)employment
encourage	encouragement
enjoy	enjoyment
entertain	entertainment
excite	excitement
govern	government
improve	improvement
invest	investment
involve	involvement
judge	judgement/judgment
manage	management
measure	measurement
move	movement
(re)pay	(re)payment
punish	punishment
refresh	refreshment
replace	replacement
require	requirement
retire	retirement
settle	settlement
treat	treatment

-ness

Adjective	Noun
(un)aware	(un)awareness
careless	carelessness
close	closeness
(un)conscious	(un)consciousness
deaf	deafness
eager	eagerness
(in)effective	(in)effectiveness
(un)friendly	(un)friendliness
great	greatness
hard	hardness
hopeless	hopelessness
(un)selfish	(un)selfishness
serious	seriousness
stiff	stiffness
thorough	thoroughness
tired	tiredness
useful	usefulness
weak	weakness

-ship

Person	Abstract noun
champion	championship
companion	companionship
friend	friendship
leader	leadership
member	membership
owner	ownership
partner	partnership
scholar	scholarship*
sponsor	sponsorship**

*scholarship
money given to someone to help pay for their studies

**sponsorship
money given to someone/an organization to help pay for something, eg an event

Adjective	Noun
hard	hardship

-sis

Verb	Noun
diagnose	diagnosis
emphasize	emphasis

-sion

Verb	Noun
collide	collision
erode	erosion
exclude	exclusion
expand	expansion
include	inclusion
persuade	persuasion
supervise	supervision

-son

Verb	Noun
compare	comparison

-ation

Verb	Noun
adapt	adaptation
administer	administration
apply	application
combine	combination
compile	compilation
consider	consideration
expect	expectation
explain	explanation
identify	identification
imagine	imagination
inflame	inflammation
inform	information
inspire	inspiration
interpret	interpretation
observe	observation
prepare	preparation
present	presentation
publish	publication
(dis)qualify	(dis)qualification
realize	realization
resign	resignation
vary	variation

-tion

Verb	Noun
accommodate	accommodation
(re)act	(re)action
associate	association
collect	collection
complicate	complication
compose	composition
(dis)connect	(dis)connection
contaminate	contamination
demonstrate	demonstration
direct	direction
evolve	evolution
hesitate	hesitation
imitate	imitation
inhibit	inhibition
investigate	investigation
(de)motivate	(de)motivation
operate	operation
perceive	perception
predict	prediction
prescribe	prescription
receive	reception
recognize	recognition
reduce	reduction
repeat	repetition
(dis)satisfy	(dis)satisfaction
(re)solve	(re)solution
subscribe	subscription
substitute	substitution

-th

Adjective	Noun
broad	breadth
deep	depth
long	length
strong	strength
warm	warmth
wide	width

Verb	Noun
grow	growth

-ure

Verb	Noun
close	closure
compose	composure
depart	departure
expose	exposure
fail	failure
please	pleasure
proceed	procedure
sign	signature

-y

Adjective	Noun
difficult	difficulty
(dis)honest	(dis)honesty
poor	poverty
safe	safety
(un)certain	(un)certainty

Verb	Noun
discover	discovery
enter	entry

People

-ant

Verb	Person
apply	applicant
assist	assistant
confide	confidant(e)
consult	consultant
contest	contestant
defend	defendant
inhabit	inhabitant
occupy	occupant
participate	participant

-ar

Verb	Person
lie	liar

-ative

Verb	Person
represent	representative

-er

Verb	Person
employ	employer
lecture	lecturer
manufacture	manufacturer
present	presenter
read	reader
research	researcher
win	winner

-ian

Noun	Person
electricity	electrician
history	historian
library	librarian
mathematics	mathematician
music	musician
politics	politician

-ist

Noun	Person
bicycle	cyclist
environment	environmentalist
motor (car)	motorist
nature	naturalist
novel	novelist
psychiatry	psychiatrist
science	scientist
specialism	specialist
violin	violinist

-or

Verb	Person
act	actor
collect	collector
communicate	communicator
compete	competitor
conduct	conductor
contribute	contributor
demonstrate	demonstrator
distribute	distributor
instruct	instructor
invent	inventor
spectate	spectator

Nouns formed with *up, down, in, out, back*

up-

upbringing
upkeep
uprising
uproar
upset
upturn

down-

downfall
downpour
downside
downturn

-down

breakdown

in-

income
input
insight
intake

out-

outbreak
outburst
outcome
outline
outlook
output
outset

-out

breakout
checkout
knockout
turnout
workout

-back

comeback
drawback
feedback
setback

back-

background

Miscellaneous

Verb	Noun
behave	(mis)behaviour
choose	choice
complain	complaint
die	death
give	gift
know	knowledge
laugh	laughter
lose	loss
prove	proof
receive	receipt
respond	response
sell	sale(s)
succeed	success
think	thought
try	trial
weigh	weight

Adjective	Noun
high	height

Adjectives

-able

Verb	Adjective
accept	(un)acceptable
advise	(in)advisable
afford	affordable
agree	(dis)agreeable
apply	(in)applicable
appreciate	appreciable
approach	(un)approachable
avoid	(un)avoidable
bear	(un)bearable
believe	(un)believable
compare	(in)comparable
consider	(in)considerable
desire	(un)desirable
dispense	(in)dispensable
forget	(un)forgettable
imagine	(un)imaginable
irritate	irritable
note	notable
notice	noticeable
pay	payable
predict	(un)predictable
prefer	preferable
prevent	preventable
regret	regrettable
rely	(un)reliable
remark	(un)remarkable
respect	respectable
understand	understandable
work	(un)workable

Noun	Adjective
comfort	(un)comfortable
fashion	(un)fashionable
knowledge	knowledgeable
memory	(un)memorable
profit	(un)profitable
reason	(un)reasonable
value	valuable/invaluable*

*invaluable:
extremely useful. eg *invaluable advice/experience/help*

-ible

Noun	Adjective
access	(in)accessible
flexibility	(in)flexible
sense	(in)sensible*

Verb	Adjective
comprehend	(in)comprehensible
respond	(ir)responsible

* sensible:
showing or having good sense eg *Cycling with a broken arm is not a very sensible thing to do.*

insensible:
a unconscious
   eg *He was found drunk and insensible.*
b not caring about or unaware of
   eg *She seemed insensible to the dangers involved.*

-al

Noun	Adjective
accident	accidental
addition	additional
alphabet	alphabetical
behaviour	behavioural
centre	central
culture	cultural
ecology	ecological
emotion	(un)emotional
environment	environmental
exception	(un)exceptional
experiment	experimental
fact	factual
globe	global
intention	intentional
medicine	medicinal
method	methodical
monument	monumental
nation	national
occasion	occasional
occupation	occupational
origin	(un)original
parent	parental
person	(im)personal
practice	(im)practical
profession	(un)professional
sensation	(un)sensational
society	social
temperament	temperamental
tradition	traditional
universe	universal

-ial

Noun	Adjective
benefit	beneficial
commerce	commercial
controversy	(un)controversial
face	facial
finance	financial
industry	industrial
influence	influential
manager	managerial
matrimony	matrimonial
residence	residential
secretary	secretarial
substance	(in)substantial
territory	territorial

-ant

Verb	Adjective
ignore	ignorant
please	(un)pleasant
rely	reliant
resist	resistant
signify	(in)significant
tolerate	(in)tolerant

-ent

Verb	Adjective
appear	apparent
confide	confident
depend	(in)dependent
differ	(in)different
insist	insistent
obey	(dis)obedient
persist	persistent
recur	recurrent

Noun	Adjective
absence	absent
(in)competence	(in)competent
(in)convenience	(in)convenient
evidence	evident
(in)frequency	(in)frequent
innocence	innocent
intelligence	intelligent
(im)patience	(im)patient
presence	present
violence	violent

-ate

Noun	Adjective
accuracy	(in)accurate
adequacy	(in)adequate
appropriacy	(in)appropriate
consideration	(in)considerate
fortune	(un)fortunate
moderation	(im)moderate

-ative

Verb	Adjective
administer	administrative
argue	argumentative
compare	comparative
consult	consultative
imagine	(un)imaginative
inform	(un)informative
prevent	preventative
provoke	provocative
represent	(un)representative

Word formation list

-ive

Verb	Adjective
act	(in)active
adopt	adoptive
appreciate	(un)appreciative
assert	(un)assertive
attend	(in)attentive
attract	(un)attractive
communicate	(un)communicative
compete	(un)competitive
conclude	(in)conclusive
construct	(un)constructive
cooperate	(un)cooperative
create	(un)creative
deceive	deceptive
decide	(in)decisive
defend	defensive
describe	descriptive
destroy	destructive
divide	divisive
explode	explosive
express	expressive
extend	extensive
impress	(un)impressive
include	inclusive
invent	inventive
offend	(in)offensive
persuade	persuasive
possess	possessive
produce	(un)productive
progress	progressive
protect	protective
receive	(un)receptive
respect	(ir)respective
respond	(un)responsive
speculate	speculative
succeed	successive
support	(un)supportive

Noun	Adjective
aggression	(un)aggressive
effect	(in)effective
expense	(in)expensive
secret	secretive
sense	(in)sensitive

-ing/-ed

The following verbs can be used to form participle adjectives
eg *worrying/worried*

alarm, amaze, amuse, annoy, astonish, bore, confuse, convince, depress, disappoint, disgust, embarrass, entertain, excite, exhaust, fascinate, frighten, frustrate, increase, interest, irritate, motivate, move, refresh, relax, satisfy, shock, surprise, terrify, threaten, thrill, tire, worry

The following –*ing* adjectives are commonly used with the nouns in brackets.

Verb	Adjective
close	closing (date)
consult	consulting (room)
recur	recurring (illness, nightmare, problem, theme)
run	running (water)
support	supporting (actor, actress, evidence, role)

-ous

Noun	Adjective
(dis)advantage	(dis)advantageous
ambition	(un)ambitious
anxiety	anxious
caution	cautious
courtesy	(dis)courteous
curiosity	curious
danger	dangerous
disaster	disastrous
glamour	(un)glamorous
hazard	hazardous
humour	humorous
luxury	luxurious
monster	monstrous
mystery	mysterious
nerve	nervous
number	numerous
poison	poisonous
religion	(ir)religious
suspicion	suspicious

Verb	Adjective
infect	infectious
vary	various

-ful/-less

Root	-ful	-less/un __ ful
beauty	beautiful	——————
care	careful	careless
cheer	cheerful	cheerless*
colour	colourful	colourless
count	——————	countless
deceit	deceitful	——————
delight	delightful	——————
effort	——————	effortless
end	——————	endless
event	eventful	uneventful
faith	faithful	unfaithful
fault	faulty	faultless
flight	——————	flightless
gratitude	grateful	ungrateful
hair	hairy	hairless
harm	harmful	harmless
heart	——————	heartless
help	helpful	helpless* / unhelpful*
home	——————	homeless
hope	hopeful	hopeless
job	——————	jobless
meaning	meaningful	meaningless
pain	painful	painless
peace	peaceful	——————
point	——————	pointless
power	powerful	powerless
price	——————	priceless*
relent	——————	relentless
resource	resourceful	unresourceful
respect	respectful	disrespectful
skill	skilful*/skilled*	unskilled
sleep	——————	sleepless
speech	——————	speechless
stress	stressful	unstressful
success	successful	unsuccessful
taste	tasty* / tasteful*	tasteless
thought	thoughtful*	thoughtless
time	——————	timeless
truth	truthful	untruthful
use	useful	useless
waste	wasteful	——————
wonder	wonderful	——————
worth	——————	worthless*
youth	youthful	——————

cheerless: used mainly to describe the weather or a room which is not bright or pleasant

helpless: unable to do anything to help or protect yourself

unhelpful: not willing to help other people

priceless: used to describe an object which has a very high value; it is worth so much money that the price cannot be calculated (compare with *worthless* below)

skilful & skilled: both can be used to describe a person who has the necessary ability, experience and / or training to do something well.
eg He's a skilful footballer. This work was done by skilled craftsmen.

skilled: can also be used to describe a job or piece of work that requires special skill and training
eg Nursing is a skilled job.

tasty: used to describe food with a strong and pleasant flavour

tasteful: used to describe clothes, decoration etc which is attractive and shows good taste

thoughtful:
a to describe a person who is quiet and serious because they are thinking about something
b to describe someone who thinks and cares about the feelings and needs of other people

worthless: used to describe an object with no value in money (compare with *priceless* above)

-ic

Noun	Adjective
allergy	allergic
drama	dramatic
optimism	optimistic
pessimism	pessimistic
science	scientific
strategy	strategic

Word formation list

-ary

Noun	Adjective
caution	cautionary
literature	literary
revolution	revolutionary

Verb	Adjective
imagine	imaginary
volunteer	(in)voluntary

-ory

Verb	Adjective
advise	advisory
celebrate	celebratory
contradict	contradictory
explain	explanatory
introduce	introductory
migrate	migratory
oblige	obligatory
prepare	preparatory
satisfy	(un)satisfactory
supervise	supervisory

-ly

Noun	Adjective
friend	(un)friendly
life	lively
time	(un)timely

-y

Noun	Adjective
chat	chatty
cloud	cloudy
ease	easy
fault	faulty
fog	foggy
frost	frosty
grass	grassy
guilt	guilty
hair	hairy
hill	hilly
mist	misty
mud	muddy
rain	rainy
rock	rocky
sleep	sleepy
sun	sunny
wealth	wealthy

Verbs

-ate

Noun	Verb
assassin	assassinate
difference	differentiate
value	evaluate
captive	captivate
dominant	dominate
valid	validate

en-

Noun	Verb
courage	encourage (discourage)
danger	endanger
force	enforce

Adjective	Verb
able	enable
large	enlarge
rich	enrich
sure	ensure

-en

Adjective	Verb
black	blacken
bright	brighten
broad	broaden
dark	darken
deaf	deafen
deep	deepen
fat	fatten
flat	flatten
hard	harden
high	heighten
long	lengthen
less	lessen
loose	loosen
red	redden
sad	sadden
sharp	sharpen
short	shorten
soft	soften
stiff	stiffen
straight	straighten
strong	strengthen
sweet	sweeten
thick	thicken
tight	tighten
weak	weaken
wide	widen
worse	worsen

Noun	Verb
threat	threaten

-ify

Noun	Verb
class	classify
example	exemplify
glory	**glorify**
identity	identify
qualification	(dis)qualify

Adjective	Verb
clear	clarify
pure	purify
simple	simplify

-ize

Noun	Verb
character	characterize
computer	computerize
emphasis	emphasize
memory	memorize
moisture	moisturize
summary	summarize
symbol	symbolize

Adjective	Verb
commercial	commercialize
familiar	familiarize
general	generalize
modern	modernize
social	socialize
special	specialize
stable	stabilize

Verbs formed with *up, down, over, under, out*

up-

update
upgrade
uphold
uproot
upset
upstage

down-

downgrade
download
downplay
downsize

over-

overcook
overhear
overload
overrule
oversleep
overtake
overthrow
overuse

under-

undercut
undergo
undertake

out-

outgrow
outlast
outlive
outnumber
outplay
outrun
outstay

Unit 1

Reading 1, page 4

CAE Part 1 Multiple matching

1 B
2 1 G   2 E   3 B   4 C   5 D   6 G
  7 B   8 D   9 A   10 B   11 C   12 E
  13 F   14 A

Vocabulary, page 6

Verb and noun collocations

1 into   2 with
3 out   4 in
5 to

Adjective and noun collocations

1
1 inside   2 resounding
3 burning   4 hard
5 terrible   6 urgent
7 heated   8 outlying

2
1 slim   2 recurrent
3 daunting   4 poor
5 overnight   6 dismal
7 lifelong   8 sporting

Word formation

1 exposure   2 proposals
3 inflexibility 4 vacancies
5 emphasis   6 requirements
7 closeness   8 shortage
9 irrelevance   10 notoriety

Language focus, page 7

Spelling

Incorrect spelling	Correct spelling
writting	writing
apeared	appeared
Loosers	Losers
wich	which
agresive	aggressive
wellfare	welfare
totaly	totally
although	although
their	there
ougth	ought
adition	addition
intervue	interview
where	were
oportunity	opportunity
impresive	impressive
pane	pain
too	to
extremly	extremely
innacuracies	inaccuracies
faithfuly	faithfully

Modal verbs: *might, could, may, can*

1
1 live here, but we never see him
2 (very) well be asked to speak French during the interview
3 not have known you were married
4 (well) have got it
5 as well sell it
6 have told me you were vegetarian
7 have been enjoying herself very much

2
1 can   2 could   3 may   4 could
5 may   6 could   7 could

English in Use, page 9

CAE Part 1 Multiple-choice cloze

1 B   2 D   3 D   4 C   5 C   6 A   7 B
8 A   9 C   10 B   11 B   12 D   13 C
14 D   15 A

Writing, page 10

CAE Part 2 Competition entries

2 B

3 Reasons: Paragraph 2
Preparations: Paragraph 3
Feelings: Paragraphs 1, 3 and 4

4 The short sentence 'But I got through it' is used for emphasis, drawing attention to the fact that despite all the nerves suffered in the lead-up to the play, the writer survived.
'Almost' is not a sentence in the true sense of the word, as it does not contain a subject or a verb. It is repeated at the very end of the answer both for emphasis and humorous effect. It provides an interesting conclusion to the article.

5 Contractions
you're, I'd, hadn't

Phrasal verbs

put themselves through such an ordeal
take up the challenge
trying out different postures
I got through it

Words linking sentences

So when I was offered the chance
When rehearsals started though
But I got through it.

Addressing the reader directly

Why, you might ask, would anyone willingly put themselves through such an ordeal?

6 *Possible answers*
Past perfect: *I'd been involved, I'd only ever been given*
Past simple: *I was offered, I felt*
Past continuous: *my motivation was beginning to run low, my legs were trembling*

Useful language

Nervous	Happy	Sad
have butterflies in your stomach	be over the moon	be/feel down
be/get uptight	be/feel on top of the world	feel sorry for yourself
be a bundle of nerves	be on a high	be in low spirits
be/feel panicky	be as pleased as punch	

130

Reading, page 12

CAE Part 3 Multiple choice

1 A **2** B **3** C **4** D **5** B **6** A

Vocabulary, page 13

Changes

1

1 transferred	2 shifted
3 adapted	4 altered

2

1 B **2** D **3** A **4** C **5** A

3

1 scene	2 heart
3 pace	4 direction
5 fortunes	6 condition
7 law	8 attitudes

Language focus, page 15

1

1 used to	2 was (still) eating
3 met	4 have eaten
5 have seen/saw	6 had caught
7 have stayed	8 hadn't given
9 have done	10 to sit

2
A
1 has been putting
2 has managed
3 has met
4 believed/used to believe
5 asked/used to ask/would ask
6 have changed
7 said
8 lit/used to light/would light

B
1 went
2 saw/had seen
3 was working/worked
4 booked/had booked
5 Having washed
6 had just landed
7 had been experiencing
8 would take/was going to take
9 spent
10 didn't arrive
11 had been sitting
12 had left/would be leaving/was going to leave/ was leaving
13 had ever had
14 would be/was going to be

English in Use, page 16

CAE Part 3 Error correction

1	Steiff drew	2	✔
3	Teddy?	4	✔
5	tied	6	✔
7	shopkeepers	8	Bears".
9	Americans	10	factory
11	✔	12	which
13	✔	14	building
15	display	16	fifteen

CAE Part 4 Word formation

1	safety	2	historians
3	existence	4	symbolized/symbolised
5	accidental	6	unknown
7	mysteriously	8	readers
9	latest	10	beautifully
11	adaptation	12	dissatisfaction
13	starring	14	sales
15	variation		

Writing, page 18

CAE Part 1 Formal and informal letters

2

1	satisfaction	2	deal
3	knowledge	4	explanations
5	attention	6	improve
7	Firstly	8	departure
9	failed	10	addition
11	illness	12	Finally
13	discover/learn/hear	14	arrival
15	entrance/admission		

Unit 3

Reading, page 20

CAE Part 2 Gapped text

1 = E   2 = A   3 = B   4 = C   5 = F   6 = D
G = not used

Vocabulary, page 22

Adjective and noun collocations

1 *Across:* **3** ambition **5** aroma **6** method **8** success **11** change **12** challenge
Down: **1** changes **2** odour **4** information **7** failure **9** chance **10** smell

2 *Possible answers (see also Wordlist on pages 209–211 of the Coursebook)*
lifelong/secret **ambition**
pleasant/sweet **aroma**
convenient/efficient **method**
huge/great **success**
refreshing/pleasant **change**
formidable/major **challenge**
far-reaching/significant **changes**
acrid/stale **odour**
biased/reliable **information**
total/continued **failure**
slight/remote **chance**
faint/rancid **smell**

Verb and noun collocations

1

2	an ambition	3	information
4	a challenge	5	change
6	a problem	7	a possibility
8	a smell		

2

2	pursue	3	gathering
4	presents	5	resisting
6	resolved	7	looking into
8	get rid of		

Word formation

1	ignorant	2	countless
3	inaccessible	4	numerous
5	surprisingly	6	literary
7	unsuccessful	8	comparative
9	dramatically	10	introductory

Language focus, page 24

1

1 had seen/watched
2 rather/sooner have
3 been for
4 have worn/taken
5 to have
6 Had I
7 you had, would/could have
8 might/would not/never, been driving/travelling

2

1 C	2 A, B, C
3 B	4 A, B, C
5 A, B	6 B, C
7 C	8 A, C

English in Use, page 25

CAE Part 1 Multiple-choice cloze

1 D   2 C   3 A   4 C   5 B   6 B   7 D
8 D   9 A   10 B   11 C   12 C   13 B
14 B   15 A

Writing, page 26

CAE Part 1 Formal letters

A

2 Comments 1 and 4 ('the ones they've got are pretty old and in very poor condition' and 'They could do with some more reference books …')
3 Comment 2 ('We don't need any more sports facilities .'.)
4 Class survey
5 Class survey

B

2 is more appropriate: it summarizes the information from the survey as instructed, and focuses only on those aspects which are of most relevance to the task.
1 merely copies the information from the survey, using the same words.

C

1 period   *when fewest people go*
2 Priority   *more important to have a decent library*
3 journey   *not everyone can get there easily*
4 claim   *nonsense!*
5 evidence   *where's the proof?*

Reading, page 28

CAE Part 3 Multiple choice

1 B   2 B   3 D   4 A   5 C   6 A   7 D

Vocabulary, page 30

A Adjectives of personality

1 industrious	2 slapdash
3 approachable	4 conceited
5 attentive	6 single-minded
7 trustworthy	8 domineering

B Time

1 for	2 out
3 aside	4 up
5 of	6 in
7 at	8 to
9 on	10 off

C Skills

Across: 8 technical 10 communication 11 personal
Down: 1 telephone 2 organizational 3 practical
5 business 6 secretarial 7 managerial 9 language

Language focus, page 31

Gerunds and infinitives

1 refusal to work overtime surprised me.
2 isn't worth (you/your) reading that book.
3 you like me to carry your bag for you?
4 made a big/great effort to give up smoking.
5 appreciate you/your coming at such short notice.
6 couldn't help laughing when he said that.
7 had better leave now if you don't want to miss/or/otherwise you'll miss the bus.
8 have difficulty remembering names.
9 were made to clean up the mess.
10 to him/his being treated so badly.

English in Use, page 32

CAE Part 2 Open cloze

1 the	2 to
3 although/though/while/whilst	4 most
5 has	6 such
7 in	8 because/as
9 at	10 once
11 is	12 on
13 one	14 not
15 less	

CAE Part 4 Word formation

1 representatives	**2** leadership
3 communicator	**4** attendance
5 preferable/preferred	**6** competitive
7 closing	**8** explanation
9 resulting	**10** inability
11 harmful	**12** tendency
13 behavioural	**14** concentrating
15 tiredness	

Writing, page 34

CAE Part 2 Reports

2 The correct order and possible headings are:
- **4** Introduction
- **2** General background
- **1** The effect of the car
- **5** The effect of television
- **3** Future developments

3

Language used to compare the past and the present

Street games ... are no longer such a common sight.
cycling ... is becoming less attractive
youngsters now spend more time in the home ...
The main difference between now and twenty years
ago ...
the increased wealth and greater amount of free time available ...
Where previously whole families ..., now children ...
Courting couples rarely go ballroom dancing ... as they once did; instead ...

Language used to make future predictions

Teenagers and people in their twenties may well spend ...
They might even begin to wish ...

Different ways of referring to young people

young people
our youth
teenagers and people in their twenties
children
courting couples

Different ways of referring to free time

free time
spare time
leisure time

4

but two other developments have restricted the nature and quality of leisure time activities
Sadly, youngsters now spend more time in the home they stay in to watch television, or perhaps worse, attend wild pop concerts or parties, where they dance in uncontrolled ways

5

a The growth in the popularity of the car
b particularly with the construction of motorways
c the increased wealth and greater amount of free time available to young people

Unit 5

Reading, page 36

CAE Part 3 Multiple choice

1 C   2 A   3 B   4 C   5 D   6 C

Vocabulary, page 37

Adjective and noun collocations

1

1 love	2 feelings
3 couple	4 relationship
5 friend	6 family
7 argument	8 tension

2

1 love-hate	2 pointless
3 unrequited	4 mixed
5 immediate	6 close

Verbs

1 **a** called   **b** call
2 **a** fell   **b** fell
3 **a** took   **b** takes
4 **a** turned   **b** turn

Language focus, page 38

Relative clauses

1 who	2 which
3 which	4 whose
5 where	6 why
7 who	8 that/who

Alternatives to relative clauses

1 Venus and Serena Williams – tennis players (Maud Watson beat her sister Lilian in the first women's final in 1884).

2 Michael and Ralf Schumacher – Formula 1 racing drivers

3 The Marx brothers – actors. Groucho (3b), Chico, Harpo, Zeppo and Gummo

4 Janet and Michael Jackson – popstars. The group was The Jackson 5 (later The Jacksons).

5 JF and RF Kennedy – US politicians. Robert was himself assassinated while campaigning for the presidency in 1968.

2

1 **b** the *one who* collected the winner's trophy

2 **a** a go-kart *which was* powered by a lawnmower engine.

   b the first *one who phoned* his mother.

3 **a** Monkey Business, Duck Soup and A Night at the Opera, all *of which were* released/*which were* all released in the 1930s.

   b a moustache *which was* painted on with black greasepaint

4 **a** Fans *who were* hoping to see Janet

   b a group *which comprised* himself and four of his eight brothers and sisters.

5 **a** the youngest man *who was* ever elected President, he was also the youngest *one who died*.

   b Robert, *who was* known affectionately as Bobby, had evidence *which backed up/could back up* his suspicions

English in Use, page 39

CAE Part 3 Error correction

1 explains,	2 address
3 within	4 don't
5 ✔	6 this will
7 ✔	8 current
9 me.	10 ✔
11 great	12 swapped/swopped
13 exotic	14 sports
15 performance	16 bar will

CAE Part 5 Register transfer

1 worried/preoccupied
2 a lot/a few
3 (ever) listens
4 always/forever/continually
5 classmates/neighbours/partners/peers
6 gets on
7 rude/impolite
8 happen/take place
9 end/stop/finish
10 a couple
11 called/been calling
12 to lose
13 talk about/talk through/talk over/go through

Writing, page 41

CAE Part 1 Character reference and note

2

The character reference focuses more on Anna Kaufmann's negative points and the overall impression would be rather negative.
The note is over twice the length of that indicated in the task.

3

a F

The personnel manager asks the writer to 'include at least one weakness'. It is neither necessary nor appropriate to mention all of those in the input material.

b T

The long central paragraph - more than half of the character reference - is given over entirely to the friend's negative qualities. However, the overall impression you wish to create is positive: the handwritten note *'definitely'* in the input material confirms this. The positive points are merely listed in the first and last paragraphs.

c F

The note is appropriately informal, but the character reference should be written in a more formal register.

d T

Character reference: the references to chatting in lessons at school and the friend's sister in Limerick are irrelevant.
Note: the first sentence is unnecessarily detailed and long (over 40 words). Mention of the inclusion of negative points is not entirely irrelevant, but given the word limit, it should be briefer.

e T

This is particularly the case in the character reference: eg *She's a really nice, friendly person; She can be a bit sensitive to criticism and sometimes she's too talkative; she can lose her temper unexpectedly.*

4

often does her own thing without considering others/very independent-minded
sensitive to criticism/really nice – very friendly
sometimes too talkative!/great talker

Unit 6

Reading, page 44

CAE Part 4 Multiple matching

1

b The writer reports what the pupils and teachers have said about Henry (for example: undisputed star/soulful eyes/a pupil's best friend/a super dog/a calming influence etc). She does not use any language to argue or disagree with these descriptions.

2

1 F	2 D	3 G	4 A	5/6 B,F in any order
7 C	8 A	9/10 C,E in any order
11 D	12 A	13 B	14 E
15 D	16 G	17 E	18 G

Vocabulary, page 46

A Sleep

1 to	2 up
3 through	4 into
5 over	6 on
7 off	8 from

B Abilities

1 d 2 b 3 e 4 a 5 f 6 c

C Adjectives in film reviews

1 unconvincing	2 innovative
3 clichéd	4 gripping
5 over-hyped	6 moving
7 excruciating	8 stunning

Language focus, page 47

1

1 a 2 b 3 b 4 a 5 b

2

1 is understood to be planning a takeover bid for its rival
2 are said (by police) to have taken place on Monday
3 motorcyclist is believed to have been travelling at over 100 miles per hour
4 were thought to be/to have been responsible for the outbreak of flu
5 was alleged to have lied in order to protect her boyfriend
6 my camera stolen last weekend
7 to get/have your eyes tested
8 got my foot stuck in the hole

135

English in Use, page 48

CAE Part 2 Open cloze

1	being/getting	2	do
3	who/that	4	only/just/merely
5	themselves	6	to
7	is/gets	8	as/being
9	from	10	with
11	for/without	12	be/get
13	Not/Hardly	14	at
15	while/whilst/when		

CAE Part 4 Word formation

1	Researchers	2	greatness
3	variety	4	containing
5	comparison	6	responses
7	noticeably	8	recognition
9	unreliable	10	knowledge

Writing, page 49

CAE Part 2 Article

1

Version B. Whilst the general content is the same, it is far more interesting to read than A, and the language used is richer and more varied. For example, compare *got good marks, good at sport* and *sports facilities were very good* in version A, with *academic achievement was high, talented young sportsmen* and *extensive sports facilities* in version B. The opening paragraph in B engages the reader's interest and the closing paragraph leaves the reader with something to think about (see 3 B below).

2

a Paragraph 3

b Paragraphs 1, 2 and 4

c Paragraph 1: *the secondary school I had the misfortune to attend*

Paragraph 2: *The teacher was the source of all knowledge etc*

... trapped in a time bubble of passive learning and iron discipline

Paragraph 4: the whole paragraph

d Paragraph 2: *Whilst the trend up and down the country* etc

Paragraph 3: *Indeed, unlike most other schools at the time ...*

3

A

1

2 Teaching and learning methods

3 Discipline

4 Range of subjects

5 Academic achievement

6 Facilities

7 Extra-curricular activities

2 All except 'Range of subjects'.

B

1 A quotation from a teacher is used to engage the reader's interest in the first sentence.

Rhetorical questions, followed by a brief answer from the writer, are used in the final paragraph to leave the reader something to think about.

2

1 A fact or statistic

2 A question

3 A story

4 An unusual statement

5 A comparison

Unit 7

Reading, page 52

CAE Part 2 Gapped text

1

1 D   2 E   3 A   4 B   5 G   6 C

F = not used

2

set out – arranged or displayed in writing

set up – started running a business

3

2 b   3 e   4 a   5 g   6 f   7 d

Vocabulary, page 54

Phrasal verbs

1 **a** brought
  b bring
2 **a** worn
  b wear
3 **a** got
  b get
4 **a** broke
  b break
5 **a** put
  b put
6 **a** come
  b come

Word formation

1

-en	*en-*
deafen	encourage
heighten	endanger
deepen	enrich
sadden	enforce
broaden	

2

1 heightened   2 deepening
3 encouraging   4 endangered
5 enforcement   6 saddened
7 broadens/broadened, enriches/enriched
8 deafening

Language focus, page 55

Reported speech

1 The following words should be crossed out:

1 refused/offered
2 denied/claimed
3 accused/complained
4 persuaded/encouraged
5 complimented/congratulated
6 suggested/argued
7 urge/convince
8 told/assured
9 suggested/proposed
10 ordered/insisted

2

1 **a** he would cut
  b to cut
2 **a** thought I should take
  b (that) I (should) take/(that) I took
3 **a** they had to leave
  b them to leave
4 **a** he had always loved
  b having always loved
5 **a** hadn't stolen it
  b having stolen it/stealing it
6 **a** was paid
  b to have been paid
7 **a** she could take
  b his name should not
8 **a** had been abducted
  b have been abducted

English in Use, page 57

CAE Part 3 Error correction

1 own   2 which
3 at   4 have
5 like   6 ✔
7 if   8 ✔
9 had   10 ✔
11 was   12 only
13 ✔   14 most
15 also   16 being

CAE Part 6 Gapped text

1 F   2 H   3 B   4 G   5 D   6 C

Writing, page 58

CAE Part 2 Review

2 Yes

3

1 title		**2** performance	
3 nomination		**4** set	
5 scenes		**6** climax	
7 score		**8** action	
9 insight		**10** lines	

4

extremely powerful acting performance

well-deserved Oscar nomination

the boxing scenes are entirely convincing

(the film builds up to) a dramatic climax

(Michael Mann's) expert direction

the moving musical score

(one of the most) memorable moments (of the film)

(it provides) a fascinating insight (into)

witty lines

5

is reason enough to see the film

don't be put off if you're not a boxing fan

There's something for everyone in the film

will have you laughing out loud

Unit 8

Reading, page 60

CAE Part 3 Multiple choice

1

1 A   **2** D   **3** C   **4** A   **5** C   **6** B

2

1 c   **2** a   **3** b

3

1 H   **2** D   **3** H   **4** H   **5** D

4

a underhand	**b** devious	**c** reputable
d candid	**e** straight	

Vocabulary, page 62

Verbs formed with *up, down, over* and *under*

1

1 uphear

2 overgo

3 underroot

4 uprule

5 downhold

2

1 uphold, overrule

2 undergo

3 update, upgrade

4 undercut

5 downplay

Adjectives formed with *in, off, on, out* and *over*

1 oncoming

2 ongoing

3 outlying

4 off-duty

5 inborn

Plans

1

1 emergency	**2** devious
3 impracticable	**4** carry out
5 put forward	**6** shelve

2

1 impracticable	**2** emergency
3 devious	**4** shelved
5 carrying out	**6** put forward

Computer technology

1

A

1 c mouse mat

2 d keyboard

3 a laptop

4 e disk drive

5 b webcam

B

1 d chat room

2 e home page

3 a search engine

4 c service provider

5 b bulletin board

2

mouse mat 6

keyboard 8

laptop 1

disk drive 9

webcam 2

chat room 3

home page 10

search engine 5

service provider 7

bulletin board 4

Language focus, page 64

Talking about the future
1 C   2 C   3 B   4 C   5 D   6 C   7 A   8 B

Determiners
1 no other
2 every other
3 Every few
4 another two
5 quite a few / quite a lot of
6 quite some
7 not much
8 some three

English in Use, page 65

CAE Part 2 Open cloze
1 the   2 of   3 a   4 over   5 them   6 into
7 for   8 Although/Though/While/Whilst/Whereas
9 by   10 that/which   11 its   12 us   13 to
14 at   15 on/upon

CAE Part 6 Gapped text
1 H   2 C   3 E   4 F   5 D   6 I

Unit 9

Reading, page 68

CAE Part 1 Multiple matching
1 C   2 A   3 B   4 D   5 B   6 D   7 C
8 A   9 B   10 D   11 C   12 A   13 B

Vocabulary, page 70

Doing things alone
1 c   2 g   3 f   4 d   5 b   6 a   7 h   8 e

Criticism
1
1 constructive   2 valid
3 upset by   4 arouse
5 respond to   6 draw

2
1 A   2 B   3 D   4 C

Word formation
1
1 composure   2 hardship
3 supporting   4 identity
5 entry

2
1 winning entry
2 Supporting Actress
3 a case of mistaken identity
4 regained his composure
5 caused considerable hardship

Language focus, page 71

Creating emphasis
1
1 have   2 what
3 because   4 and
5 it   6 so

English in Use, page 72

CAE Part 1 Multiple-choice cloze
1 A   2 B   3 B   4 D   5 A   6 C   7 D   8 C
9 B   10 B   11 A   12 D   13 B   14 B   15 D

CAE Part 5 Register transfer
1 opportunity   2 range of/variety of
3 disappointed   4 reservation for
5 punctually at   6 include
7 Discounts are   8 provided/providing
9 pensioners/senior   10 advance
  citizens   12 departure
11 be cancelled
13 full refund

Writing, page 74

CAE Part 1 Report
2
1 F: the task asks for 'some of the main positive and negative aspects of the programme' and instructs you to use the information 'appropriately'.
2 T: and other plans might also be acceptable eg including one or more recommendations in each section (Social events, Cultural events and Weekend excursions).
3 F: the inclusion of headings is a useful and sometimes desirable way of organising ideas in reports.
4 T: see page 221 of the Grammar reference in the Coursebook for the grammar of recommend, advise and suggest
5 T: perhaps the most usual register for a report is a formal one, but this is not an absolute requirement for this particular task. Consistency of register, however, is a requirement for all reports.

Unit 10

Reading, page 76

CAE Part 1 Multiple matching

1

1 C 2 D 3 A 4 B 5 C 6 B 7 D
8 B 9 A 10 C 11 D 12 A 13 B
14 C 15 D 16 A

2

1 come(s) first 2 comes to
3 came to a head 4 come and go
5 coming to an end

Vocabulary, page 78

1

A	B
1 owl	1 stomach
2 mouse	2 leaves
3 bee	3 drum
4 dog	4 music
5 lion	5 floorboards

2

1 C 2 A 3 B 4 D 5 D
6 B 7 D 8 A 9 B 10 D

Language focus, page 79

Participle clauses

1 'Lord of the Rings: Return of the King' won 11 Oscars, *equalling* the record held by 'Ben Hur' and 'Titanic' for the highest number of Academy Awards.

2 *Having* finally *discovered* where the leak was, we called in a plumber.

3 The school now has 1,254 students, *representing* a 6% increase on last year's figure.

4 Part of the stadium roof collapsed, *injuring* six spectators.

5 *Not being* a parent, I can take my holidays whenever I like.

6 The team has had a disastrous season so far, *winning/having won* only three of its last sixteen games.

7 Our parents *having gone* away for the weekend, my brother and I had a party.

8 *Walking* home from school yesterday, I bumped into Alex.

English in Use, page 79

CAE Part 3 Error correction

1 also	2 If
3 ✔	4 those
5 on	6 ✔
7 ✔	8 out
9 it	10 more
11 only	12 of
13 another	14 that
15 soon	16 ✔

CAE Part 1 Multiple-choice cloze

1 C 2 D 3 A 4 A 5 A 6 B 7 C
8 D 9 D 10 D 11 C 12 B 13 A
14 C 15 C

CAE Part 4 Word formation

1 privacy	2 satisfying
3 ensure	4 freely
5 safety	6 procedure(s)
7 setting(s)	8 neighbourhoods
9 guaranteed	10 Costing
11 fitted	12 uninterrupted
13 luxurious	14 equipped
15 running	

Writing, page 82

CAE Part 2 Contribution to a brochure

2

These are generally situated well away from busy towns to end of paragraph
can pay as little as 300 Euros for a week in the high season
but accommodates up to 6 people
If comfort is a major factor
with all the benefits of a five-star hotel to end of paragraph
if you really want to pamper yourself

3

In the lower price bracket
Prices vary depending on
can pay as little as 300 Euros
A rather more expensive option is
works out at about 90 Euros
money is no object
at the upper end of the price range
costing anywhere between 150 and 300 Euros

4

offering, designed, depending, located, costing

Unit 11

Reading, page 84

CAE Part 4 Multiple matching

1 A   2 C   3 A   4 C   5 B   6 C   7 D
8 F   9 B   10 C   11 A   12 E   13 D
14 D   15 E   16 A   17 E   18 F

Vocabulary, page 86

Sight

1 visibility	2 eyesight, vision
3 eye	4 look
5 sight	6 full
7 closer	8 naked
9 keep	10 catch

Read and write

1

1 off	2 up
3 out	4 into

2

a 4   b 2   c 1   d 3

Language focus, page 87

Inversion

1

1 no	2 have
3 are	4 but
5 Not	6 Under
7 when/if	8 will/can
9 Only	10 On

2

Possible answers

1 had I got	2 she saw
3 have I had	4 will I allow
5 had he started	6 did I think
7 will I follow	8 did they realize

English in Use, page 88

CAE Part 5 Register transfer

1 ages	2 display/show/view
3 present	4 put
5 outside	6 long as
7 such	8 the chance/the opportunity
9 dress	10 to pay
11 weekdays	12 at least
13 look at	

CAE Part 6 Gapped text

1 F   2 B   3 I   4 C   5 G   6 D

Writing, page 90

CAE Part 2 Leaflets

1

a Do your homework
b Practice makes perfect
c The day of the interview

2

1 The best place to look is
2 It's also worthwhile to
3 it's far more advisable to
4 Make a special point of rehearsing
5 It would be a mistake to
6 it's always wise to

3

A Gathering ideas

i

1 Listening
2 Vocabulary, Grammar
3 Reading, Vocabulary, Writing, Speaking
4 Writing
5 Speaking

ii

Answers will vary.

B Organizing ideas

b would be inappropriate

Unit 12

Reading, page 92

CAE Part 2 Gapped text

1

1 = H   2 = E   3 = B   4 = G   5 = C   6 = A
7 = D   F = not used

2

1 tap, sparkling	2 drinking
3 rain	4 salt
5 running	6 flood

Vocabulary, page 94

Verb and noun collocations

1

1 on friends	2 the truth
3 someone a favour	4 an effort
5 a lie	6 birth

2

1 pay, attention	2 denied, rumours
3 welcomed, decision	4 wish, harm
5 lead, life	6 meet, expectations
7 kept, temper	8 meet, deadline
9 denied, access	10 wish, luck

Approximation

1 something	2 so
3 Very	4 Just
5 round	6 upwards
7 some	8 something

Language focus, page 95

Conjunctions

Possible answers

1 I enjoyed the film 'Ali' even though I don't like boxing.
2 They won the game despite the fact that two of their players were sent off.
3 We'd better/ We ought to phone her, otherwise she'll worry about us.
4 However I comb it, my hair always looks a mess!
5 I'll leave the plate there in case you want some more later.
6 We spoke very quietly so as not to wake up my dad.

Modal verbs

1 permitted	2 forbidden
3 recommended	4 required
5 obliged	6 supposed
7 presumed	8 obligatory

English in Use, page 96

CAE Part 4 Word formation

1 discovery	2 erosion
3 unreliable	4 threatened
5 ecological	6 endangered
7 survival	8 largest
9 length	10 densely
11 describing	12 hairless
13 existence	14 mistaken
15 steadily	

CAE Part 6 Gapped text

1 E   2 I   3 A   4 G   5 C   6 F

CAE Part 3 Error correction

1 Bubbler, an	2 oxygen
3 ✔	4 investigate. Tom
5 accidentally	6 ✔
7 admit that	8 ✔
9 its	10 pair
11 see	12 thought
13 released	14 along
15 Wednesday	16 ✔

Writing, page 98

CAE Part 2 Proposal

1

1 This has led to	2 therefore
3 also	4 instead
5 Whilst	6 As well as
7 Clearly	8 Finally
9 In order to	10 as

2

a substantial proportion of the budget should therefore be allocated to
money might also be spent on
funds would also need to be set aside for
some of the budget should be devoted to

Unit 13

Reading, page 100

CAE Part 2 Gapped text

1

1 = E **2** = G **3** = B **4** = F **5** = D **6** = C

A = not used

2

1 revival **2** descriptions
3 rarity **4** pronouncement
5 expectations **6** turnover
7 enthusiasts **8** anxiety

Vocabulary, page 102

Phrasal verbs and prepositions

A Eating and drinking

1 off **2** down **3** at **4** up

B Deception

1 into **2** on **3** at **4** for

Expressions with *eat*

1

1 home
2 hand
3 profits
4 words
5 horse
6 bird

2

2 a **3** f **4** b **5** e **6** d

Intensifiers

1 b **2** e **3** f **4** h **5** d **6** a **7** g **8** c

Language focus, page 103

Comparisons

1 ... I worked as a security guard ...
2 ... attracted her to him as/but his warm ...
3 ... anywhere near as hard ...
4 ... a great deal more convenient ...
5 ... the film was so hugely successful ...
6 ... the same way as certain types ...

English in Use, page 104

CAE Part 1 Multiple-choice cloze

1 C **2** C **3** B **4** D **5** D **6** C **7** A
8 B **9** D **10** A **11** B **12** C **13** D
14 C **15** B

CAE Part 4 Word formation

1 gathering **2** imaginative
3 proof **4** unattractive
5 refreshingly **6** combinations
7 heights **8** medicinal
9 lower **10** providing
11 inflammation **12** stiffness
13 mobility **14** reduced
15 researchers/researches

CAE Part 2 Open cloze

1 up **2** out
3 to **4** with
5 they **6** into
7 them **8** as
9 while/whilst **10** has
11 of **12** as
13 are **14** to
15 no

Writing, page 106

CAE Part 1 Formal letter and article

Possible paragraph plans

Letter

Paragraph 1
Thank manager for:
a friendliness of service
b quality of food

Paragraph 2
Express intention to return and make suggestions
for changes regarding:
a vegetarian option
b wine
c seating

Paragraph 3
Suitable closing

Article

Paragraph 1
Introduction: what, when, where, why
Emphasize success of the evening

Paragraph 2
Comment enthusiastically on:
a Mix of levels and social interaction (including
    ordering of food in English)
b Quality of food – give examples

Paragraph 3
Encourage students to participate in future evenings
Re-emphasize benefits

Unit 14

Reading, page 108

CAE Part 4 Multiple matching

1 I   2 H   3 / 4 / 5 C, G, I in any order
6 D   7 E   8 A   9 C   10 B
11 / 12 G, H in any order   13 B
14 / 15 / 16 F, G, H in any order   17 I
18 / 19 / 20 A, D, H in any order   21 B   22 F

Vocabulary, page 110

Money

1 counterfeit
2 pocket
3 housekeeping
4 ransom
5 redundancy
6 sponsorship

Verbs usually associated with money

1
1 C   2 B   3 C   4 A   5 D

2
1 pay   2 owe   3 lend   4 save   5 borrow

3
1 owe, an apology   2 pay, respects
3 borrowed, word   4 owed, a favour
5 paying, a compliment

Language focus, page 111

Noun phrases

1
1 sign   2 matter
3 grain, pack   4 sense
5 state   6 source
7 depths, height   8 chances

2
1 can of beer   2 door handle
3 a scrap of evidence   4 pieces of advice
5 three-page essay   6 a week's work
7 mountain tops   8 last April's edition

CAE Part 2 Open cloze

1 if/though   2 to
3 there   4 in
5 once, when, immediately, as   6 one
7 of   8 out
9 is   10 spite
11 being   12 on
13 what   14 of/for/with
15 their

CAE Part 3 Error correction

1 friends   2 millionaires
3 them on   4 ✔
5 their   6 ✔
7 cautious   8 says: "It's
9 decision   10 account
11 advice. Even   12 time to
13 ✔   14 planning
15 to   16 professional

CAE Part 5 Register transfer

1 range of (*not* variety of as various *appears in the note*)
2 meet/fulfil/suit the
3 access
4 to another
5 withdraw
6 provided/providing/on condition
7 a visit
8 minimum
9 of identity
10 credit
11 lasts
12 (any) delay
13 assistance

Writing, page 114

Key vocabulary

Task 1
1
1 c   2 e   3 a   4 b   5 d

2
1 Tiles   2 Power lines   3 Families
4 Roads   5 Crops

Task 2
1 installed **b**   2 pedestrianized **e**
3 demolished **d**   4 built **a**   5 introduced **c**

Task 3
1 boasts   2 entitles   3 provides   4 organizes
5 keeps

Task 4
1 strain   2 deadlines   3 duties   4 morale
5 effectiveness